Grids and Service-Oriented Architectures for Service Level Agreements

Philipp Wieder • Ramin Yahyapour
Wolfgang Ziegler
Editors

Grids and Service-Oriented Architectures for Service Level Agreements

 Springer

Editors
Philipp Wieder
TU Dortmund University
IT & Media Center
Service Computing Group
44221 Dortmund
Germany
philipp.wieder@udo.edu

Ramin Yahyapour
TU Dortmund University
IT & Media Center
Service Computing Group
44221 Dortmund
Germany
ramin.yahyapour@udo.edu

Wolfgang Ziegler
Fraunhofer-Gesellschaft
Institute for Algorithms and
Scientific Computing SCAI
Schloss Birlinghoven
53754 Sankt Augustin
Germany
wolfgang.ziegler@scai.fraunhofer.de

—

ISBN 978-1-4899-7368-9   ISBN 978-1-4419-7320-7 (eBook)
DOI 10.1007/978-1-4419-7320-7
Springer New York Dordrecht Heidelberg London

Printed on acid-free paper

Springer is part of Springer Science+Business Media (www.springer.com)

Contents

Foreword

This book contains the proceedings of the 2nd *Workshop on Service Level Agreements in Grids*, which was held in conjunction with the IEEE GRID 2009 Conference on October 13, 2009, and the proceedings of the Dagstuhl seminar *Service Level Agreements in Grids* organized in March 2009. Furthermore, this book constitutes the 13th volume of the CoreGRID book series.

CoreGRID was and is the Network of Excellence in Grid and P2P technologies funded by the European 6th Framework Programme. While the funding period as a project ended in 2008, one of great successes of CoreGRID is its sustainability. The network continued to successfully collaborate as an effective think tank in the area of Grids, distributed computing platforms and Cloud Computing. Meanwhile, the activities were supported by ERCIM as a working group on Grids, P2P and Service computing, retaining the name of CoreGRID. This also ensures sustainability of the network, maintaining and extending the active collaboration within the European Grid and SOA research community.

Being personally involved in the activities of the CoreGRID Institute on Resource Management and Scheduling, I felt privileged by the possibilities in collaborating with so many excellent partners. The continuous interest in research collaborations lead to fruitful and encouraging discussions. This demonstrates that CoreGRID achieved its goal to form a vivid and sustainable European Network of Excellence.

One outcome of these collaborations is the organization of this workshop and this seminar, and eventually the creation of this book. The proceedings show the ongoing research activities around service level agreements which are considered one of the crucial hot topics in managing services and infrastructures. The proceedings also highlight that the once very focused field of Grids extends its scope and includes now service-oriented and Cloud infrastructures as well.

I hope you enjoy the reading of the book, which is the joint work of many people. Thus, I would like to express my gratitude to all people involved in the workshop and editing of the book.

Ramin Yahyapour, CoreGRID Institute lead

Preface

The ERCIM CoreGRID working group includes a large number of European scientists working to achieve high-level research objectives in Grid and Peer-to-Peer systems. The working group brings together a critical mass of well-established researchers from more than forty European institutions active in the fields of distributed systems and middleware, models, algorithms, tools and environments.

Guarantees for quality of service in Distributed Computing Infrastructures like Grid and Clouds have turned out to be a critical as the different technology stacks became more mature and operational for production usage. The integration service-oriented architecture concepts in the Grid computing model and the growing impact of Cloud Computing put in place new technological solutions in the world of service-oriented architectures. Service-oriented Grids provide effective solutions in science and business as they offer interoperable high-performance systems for handling data- and compute-intensive distributed applications. In parallel, new methods and technologies became necessary allowing to negotiate and agree on the quality of services leading to electronic Service Level Agreements (SLAs).

This book is the 13th volume of the CoreGRID book series and it brings together scientific contributions by researchers and scientists working on different aspects of Service Level Agreements. The book includes contributions presented at the Dagstuhl Seminar *Service Level Agreements in Grids* organised between March 22nd to 27th 2009, and the IEEE *Workshop on Service Level Agreements in Grids*, which was held on October 13, 2009. This was the second workshop of its kind. The first workshop took place in Austin, Texas, US in 2007.

The objectives of both the seminar and the workshop are

- to discuss the current state of the art and new approaches in application areas that apply Service Level Agreements in the context of Grids, Clouds and distributed systems;

- to provide a forum for exchanging ideas between the different research communities focussing inter alia on agent-based approaches to SLA man-

agement, Grid economics, and SLA-based Grid resource management
and scheduling;

- to jointly work towards the development of an automated and standardized
  electronic negotiation of Service Level Agreements; and

- to provide input to the CoreGRID ERCIM Working Group.

This book contains 15 chapters. The first and the second focus on approaches
to monitor Service Level Agreements. The third chapter presents experience
made with the implementation of the Open Grid Forum's Web Services Agreement specification. The fourth chapter presents benefits of SLA-enabled resource management, while chapter five discusses the role of distributed trust
management for validating SLA choreographies.

The sixth chapter presents an overview on how Service Level Agreement
approaches are used for financial Grid applications. Chapter seven then identifies issues of SLA negotiation between autonomous agents and proposes a
notation for expressing intervals. The eighth chapter presents an overview on
the application of Service Level Agreements for Green IT. Chapter nine and
ten introduce two extensions to the Web Services Agreement standard, as there
are an approach for a multi-round negotiation extension in chapter nine and an
extension to Web Services Agreement to create open Cloud markets in chapter
ten, respectively.

Chapter eleven describes a novel approach for a service economy infrastructure, based on structured protocol descriptions and software-agent technology.
Chapter twelve gives an overview on implementation and usage of SLAs in the
European project BREIN. The thirteenth chapter discusses recent advances in
the field of negotiation and the definition of Quality of Service characteristics,
and proposes some additional features that can help both consumers and producers during the enactment of services. Chapter fourteen present first results
in establishing adaptable, versatile, and dynamic services considering negotiation boot-strapping and service mediation with a focus on meta-negotiation
and SLA mapping solutions for Grid or Cloud services representing important
prerequisites for the establishment of autonomic services. The last chapter
then deals with the negotiation of Service Level Agreements and introduces an
automated negotiation techniques between web services for the formation of
virtual organisations.

The editors would like to thank all Program Committee members who carefully reviewed the contributions to this book:

Christiana Amza, University of Toronto, Canada

Dominic Battré, TU Berlin, Germany

Francis Brazier, Vrije University, Amsterdam, The Netherlands

Asit Dan, IBM, US

Wolfgang Gentzsch, DEISA, Germany

Matthias Hovestadt, TU Berlin, Germany

Liviu Joita, Cardiff University, UK

Bastian Koller, HLRS, Stuttgart, Germany

Ioannis Kotsiopoulos, University of Manchester, UK

Gregor von Laszewski, Rochester Institute of Technology, US

Heiko Ludwig, IBM, USA

Toshi Nakata, NEC Research, Japan

Julian Padget, Bath University, UK

Shamima Paurobally, University of Liverpool, UK

Thomas Quillinan, VU University Amsterdam

Omer Rana, University of Cardiff, UK

Igor Rosenberg, ATOS Origin, Spain

Rizos Sakellariou, University of Manchester, UK

Luigi Telesca, Create-Net, Italy

Daniel Veit, University of Mannheim, Germany

Oliver Wäldrich, Fraunhofer Institute SCAI, Germany

We would like to thank all the participants for their contributions to making both the Dagstuhl seminar and the IEEE workshop a success, the workshop Program Committees for investing their time and sharing their experience, and all the authors that contributed chapters for publication in this volume. A special thank goes to the Springer staff for their assistance in editing the book.

Our thanks also go to the European Research Consortium for Informatics and Mathematics (ERCIM) for sponsoring this volume of the CoreGRID series of publications.

Philipp Wieder, Ramin Yahyapour, Wolfgang Ziegler

Contributing Authors

Rehab Alnemr Hasso Plattner Institute, Potsdam University, Germany

Jörn Altmann Seoul National University, Seoul, South-Korea

Dominic Battré Technische Universität Berlin, Germany

Victor Bayon Intel Innovation Centre, Intel Ireland Limited, Ireland

Gregor Berginc XLAB d.o.o., Slovenia

Harold Boley Institute of Information Technology, National Research Council, Canada

Ivona Brandic Institute of Information Systems, Vienna University of Technology, Austria

Frances M.T. Brazier Systems Engineering, Faculty of Technology, Policy and Management, Delft University of Technology, The Netherlands

Kassidy P. Clark Systems Engineering, Faculty of Technology, Policy and Management, Delft University of Technology, The Netherlands

Christina Cunningham Belfast e-Science Centre, The Queen's University of Belfast, UK

Schahram Dustdar Institute of Information Systems, Vienna University of Technology, Austria

Andy Edmonds Intel Innovation Centre, Intel Ireland Limited, Ireland

Henar Munoz Frutos Telefonica Investigacin y Desarrollo S.A, Spain

Manfred Grauer University of Siegen, Information Systems Institute, Germany

Primož Hadalin XLAB d.o.o., Slovenia

Irfan Ul Haq Department of Knowledge and Business Engineering, University of Vienna, Austria

Terence J Harmer Belfast e-Science Centre, The Queen's University of Belfast, UK

Matthias Hovestadt Technische Universität Berlin, Germany

Sebastian Hudert Department of Information Systems Management, University of Bayreuth, Germany

John Kennedy Intel Innovation Centre, Intel Ireland Limited, Ireland

Dalia Khader Department of Computer Science, University of Bath, UK

Bastian Koller High Performance Computing Center Stuttgart, Germany

Roland Kuebert High Performance Computing Center Stuttgart, Germany

Giuseppe Laria Centro di Ricerca in Matematica Pura ed Applicata, University of Salerno, Italy

Gregor von Laszewski Pervasive Technology Institute, Indiana University, US

Jacek Maza Intel Innovation Centre, Intel Ireland Limited, Ireland

Christoph Meinel Hasso Plattner Institute, Potsdam University, Germany

Dejan Music Institute of Information Systems, Vienna University of Technology, Austria

Ely de Oliveira Fraunhofer Institut für Techno-und Wirtschaftsmathematik, DE

Julian Padget Department of Computer Science, University of Bath, UK

Adrian Paschke Institute of Computer Science, Freie University Berlin, Germany

Shamimabi Paurobally School of Electronics and Computer Science, University of Westminster, UK

Ron Perrott Belfast e-Science Centre, The Queen's University of Belfast, UK

Franz-Josef Pfreundt Fraunhofer Institut für Techno-und Wirtschaftsmathematik, Germany

Tobias Pontz University of Siegen, Information Systems Institute, Germany

Thomas B. Quillinan D-CIS Lab, Thales Research and Technology, The Netherlands

Omer Rana School of Computer Science/Welsh eScience Centre, Cardiff University, UK

Marcel Risch Seoul National University, Seoul, South-Korea

Angela Rumpl Department of Bioinformatics, Fraunhofer Institute SCAI, Germany

Erich Schikuta Department of Knowledge and Business Engineering, University of Vienna, Austria

Sander van Splunter Systems Engineering, Faculty of Technology, Policy and Management, Delft University of Technology, The Netherlands

Yih Leong Sun Belfast e-Science Centre, The Queen's University of Belfast, UK

Axel Tenschert High Performance Computing Center Stuttgart, Germany

Oliver Wäldrich Department of Bioinformatics, Fraunhofer Institute SCAI, Germany

Lizhe Wang Pervasive Technology Institute, Indiana University, US

Martijn Warnier Systems Engineering, Faculty of Technology, Policy and Management, Delft University of Technology, The Netherlands

Peter Wright Belfast e-Science Centre, The Queen's University of Belfast, UK

Wolfgang Ziegler Department of Bioinformatics, Fraunhofer Institute SCAI, Germany

MONITORING SERVICE LEVEL AGREEMENTS IN GRIDS WITH SUPPORT OF A GRID BENCHMARKING SERVICE

Ely de Oliveira, Franz-Josef Pfreundt
Fraunhofer Institut für Techno- und Wirtschaftsmathematik
Kaiserslautern, Germany
{ely.oliveira, pfreundt}@itwm.fraunhofer.de

Abstract   As Computational Grids become more popular, a new generation of grid applications emerges, demanding strict and increasingly sophisticated guarantees of quality of service. This challenge has motivated the development of numerous technologies to enable service providers and consumers to establish Service Level Agreements (SLAs). The implementation of SLAs requires mechanisms for these agreements to be monitored and enforced, so that they can be dependable.

Most of existing SLA monitoring techniques are embedded in particular SLA specification, negotiation and management mechanisms. This poses significant limitations for their adoption in large scale, heterogeneous, decentralized grid infrastructures.

In this paper, we present how SLAs can be assessed, monitored and enforced with support of Jawari, a multi-platform, extensible and free of charge grid benchmarking service. Jawari works as an independent external entity that validates the adherence of the grid components to committed SLAs, by simply using the grid services just like an end-user would do. Doing so, it is able to observe the actual levels of quality of service the end-users are likely to experience.

Its benchmarks represent classes of grid applications with distinct requirements that expose the grid services to scenarios where the SLA is expected to be observed. Complementarily, SLA violation conditions can be routinely checked, and proper actions taken in response.

Keywords: Grid Benchmarking, SLA Monitoring, SLA Enforcement

P. Wieder et al. (eds.), *Grids and Service-Oriented Architectures for Service Level Agreements,*
DOI 10.1007/978-1-4419-7320-7_1, © Springer Science+Business Media, LLC 2010

1.   Introduction

Over the past decade, Grid Computing has emerged as a solution for the challenge of supporting applications with unprecedented requirements of scalability, computing power, platform independence, security, reliability, availability and low cost. Several middleware systems have been developed in order to make it possible for computational grids to be built [11, 14, 15, 13]. Despite their common goals, they have been developed independently, targeting different communities and use cases and this has turned them into very different solutions. Their architectures are composed by different components, relying on different protocols and algorithms, providing interfaces with different semantics and different levels of abstraction. Moreover, middleware systems are often combined with other components such as batch systems and even other middleware systems, what results in intricate infrastructures [12, 11, 13].

All this complexity undermines the ability of grid infrastructures to deliver steady platforms on which grid applications can rely. It creates an overhead that may lead services to achieve poor and unstable levels of Quality of Service (QoS). Maintenance activities may become too complex and time demanding, resulting in misconfigured components, which boosts unpredictability. Still, present day grid applications, mostly scientific, can succeed in such environment. Despite high levels of QoS are preferred and even desired by their users, such applications can tolerate some degree of lateness and occasional failures without compromising their results.

However, as identified by Bal *et al.* [3], a new generation of applications has demanded strong guarantees of QoS provision that can no longer be given by best-effort services. For example, weather services [6] and visualization applications [7] rely on obtaining results within strict time frames. Therefore, they require grid services to provide minimum levels of availability, reliability, performance and scalability that are critical for their success.

In this context, a Service Level Agreement (SLA) is a powerful instrument to describe all expectations and obligations in the relationship between service provider and customer. Applications specify their requirements and services commit themselves with the provision of a certain level of QoS. Such commitment requires the adoption of a number of techniques, including fault tolerance mechanisms, restrictions of resource usage, advanced resource reservation, performance prediction tools and monitoring services.

The implementation of SLAs requires mechanisms for these agreements to be monitored and enforced, so that they can be dependable. Most of SLA monitoring techniques developed so far are embedded in particular SLA specification, negotiation and management mechanisms [9, 8]. They often rely on specific protocols and technologies. This poses significant limitations for their widespread adoption in multi-domain, large scale, heterogeneous, decentralized grid infrastructures.

Besides, some techniques have a narrow focus and act at resource level [6]. It means that despite they may be effective in making resources work individually as expected, it does not guarantee they work as expected as a composition. For example, restrictions on the use of the network imposed by fault tolerance mechanisms may ultimately affect the application response time, regardless of how good the performance of computational resources is. Moreover, neglected components or characteristics of the system may overshadow the benefits of some techniques. For example, highly available and reliable computational resources can contribute little to the application response time in a system where the resource broker does not scale well. It is also important to keep in mind that the dynamics of the environment can not be fully tamed and also play a fundamental role in grid service provision.

In addition, each technique has a cost in terms of demanded resources, complexity injected into the system and administration activities to keep them working. Thus, they also need to be carefully chosen and their effectiveness assessed, in order to properly contribute to SLA fulfillment and make it trustworthy.

Benchmarks allow us to assess capabilities and performance of computing platforms. Hence, they would be an instrumental tool for SLA implementation, monitoring and enforcement. In this paper we present how Grid SLAs can be assessed, monitored and enforced with support of Jawari [1][1], a Grid Benchmarking and Monitoring Service. Jawari is extensible, open source, multi-platform, free of charge and requires no special configuration on the grid side. It benchmarks grid services by mimicking an end-user who submits applications of various classes, transfers files, queries information services, discovers services and so on. Doing so, it is able to capture the quality of service the end-users are likely to experience.

Jawari works as an independent external entity that allows both service providers and consumers to validate the adherence of the grid infrastructures to committed SLAs. It provides information that can be used in a variety of scenarios, including performance prediction tools, reputation based resource scheduling, resource provision accountability and billing mechanisms.

2.   Related Works

Sahai *et al.* [9] propose an architecture based on a network of communicating proxies, responsible for managing SLAs committed within their respective

---

[1]This project is sponsored by the German Research Ministry (BMBF).

administrative domains. The proxies negotiate inter-domain SLAs, collect measurements on service provision and trigger procedures for their evaluation.

In the project Sicilia [8], the SLAs are monitored throughout their life cycles by the Monitoring Service. It continuously receives QoS measurements and detects when an SLA needs attention. If so, it alerts the QoS Service that is responsible for taking due actions. The monitoring data is stored in a database that is later used by a Performance Prediction Service for identifying resources that can potentially satisfy new SLAs during their negotiation phase.

Hovestadt [6] proposes to empower the grid middleware with an SLA-aware Resource Management Service that features mechanisms like process and storage checkpointing to realize fault tolerance. This component monitors running jobs and the affected resources. In case of an error that can compromise the adherence to the SLAs, it is able to migrate the job to another matching resource.

Jawari does not claim to be self sufficient for SLA monitoring and enforcement in grids. Traditional tools such as these ones remain essential for implementing and managing the SLA mechanisms at resource and subsystem levels. It rather complements them, allowing the system as a whole to be assessed and monitored in a typically heterogeneous, multi-domain, large scale and dynamic environment.

3.   Architecture

The Jawari architecture is shown in Figure 1 and described in the following.

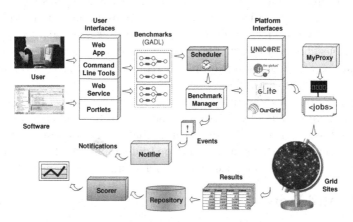

Figure 1.   Jawari Architecture

In order to achieve platform independence and extensibility, benchmark workflows and their requirements are specified in a platform independent XML-based language, so called GADL (Grid Application Description Language) [5].

In addition, each middleware system is represented by a Platform Interface object, that encapsulates all platform-specific functionalities, exposing a standard interface to the other components.

The benchmarks are orchestrated by two components. The Scheduler is responsible for their planning, according to the time constraints specified by users, while the Benchmark Manager coordinates their executions. Firstly it retrieves the benchmark GADL specification and composes workflow instances, matching their required resources with site resources, either dynamically discovered or statically informed by the user. After that, it submits the workflows to the remote sites through the suitable Platform Interface object, that parses the GADL specification into the platform-specific language. Then, it monitors the execution, collects the results and finally stores them in the Repository.

During this process, a default X509 certificate is used for authentication. Nevertheless, the user is allowed to inform the location of alternative certificates, that can be retrieved from MyProxy Servers and used for that purpose. This makes possible the evaluation of security issues such as user authorization, Virtual Organization (VO) membership and certificate renewal procedures.

The user can also subscribe to event notifications. Some events are default, such as benchmark failure and benchmark completion, but they can also be user defined logical expressions, as explained in Section 5. The events are detected by the Benchmark Manager and informed to the Notifier that sends notifications to the interested users. These notifications can be emails, HTTP requests or even SSH executions, permitting support teams to be alerted, remote procedures to be triggered and other services to react to the events.

The Scorer object is responsible for calculating performance aggregated scores. The default formula used for such calculation is explained in [1]. The user can also define his own formulas according with his own criteria. These formulas can use benchmark data as variables, such as low level measurements, normalized results and execution time.

Jawari is available through 4 user interfaces: a web site for end-users, a web service for client software, portlets for web portals and command line tools for terminal users and shell scripting. Additionally, it provides a Java API that can be used as a platform for grid application development. They make possible several usage scenarios including the integration with other tools, maintenance procedures automatization and service composition.

4.   Benchmark Suite

The current suite includes more than twenty benchmarks. Roughly speaking, they are synthetic grid applications - workflows of possibly interdependent tasks, that represent classes of real grid applications, or usual fragments of those applications. In this Section, we briefly present some examples of the suite. For a comprehensive description, please visit: *jawari.net*.

Firstly, the Single Connection benchmark focuses on grid services availability. It simply opens a connection with the target service, checking solely whether it is up and running or not.

A large group of benchmarks represents workflow patterns with different levels of complexity. The Single Task is composed by a single task with no file staging. On the other extreme, there is the Mixed Bag, composed by a collection of asymmetrically interdependent tasks. It also includes the Bag of Tasks, whose tasks are independent of each other and the Long Pipe, organized as a chain of tasks executed one after another. These benchmarks have both static and dynamic versions. The static ones define the execution place of each task, while the dynamic ones let this definition to be made by the target grid site. This group focuses on the efficiency of resource schedulers and brokers, and adopts Job turnaround time as metric.

Error Prone Task is an extension of the Single Task, whose first execution always fails. Its results are influenced by fault tolerance mechanisms such as task replication and the ability of the job manager to detect errors and repeat executions.

Another group of benchmarks focuses on service throughput. The Discovery Overload and File Transfer Overload perform a voluminous series of simple requests targeting single services from 4 distinct client machines. Complementarily, the Single File Transfer and Single Discovery perform single but complex requests from single client machines. The metric used is the number of requests attended per second.

Finally, some benchmarks focus on network bandwidth and how the middleware manages parallel large files transfers. The 3-node Probe represents the common situation when a large data file (100 Mb) is transferred from a data source host to a compute host to be processed, and a result file is transferred to a third location. The Gather Probe works in very much the same way, except that multiple files are transferred in parallel from multiple data sources to the center compute host. Similarly, the Data Job uses the user machine as both data source and result destination nodes. The metric used is Job turnaround time.

While some benchmarks are new specifications, some others are variations of previous works [2, 4], slightly modified to focus on certain grid features. Originally, they have real computation tasks as part of their workflows. In Jawari suite however, no computation is performed at all. Only lightweight command line binaries such as *echo* are executed on the target environments. Doing so, resources computational capabilities influence on the benchmark execution is significantly reduced, so that the benchmarks can better reflect other environment aspects, such as the middleware overhead. Nevertheless, the

Jawari design permits the suite to be extended and incorporate other benchmarks that might be identified as relevant for grid assessment.

The user is not limited to the standard benchmark suite. He can also write his own benchmarks in GADL and extend his assessment possibilities, including the execution of real world programs or other benchmark suites such as Linpack [19], and the query of data collected by other services such as Nagios [20]. The only constraint of this feature is that for security reasons, Jawari default certificate is used only by standard benchmarks. Therefore, the user must inform the location of alternative certificates to be used by his custom benchmarks.

5. Monitoring SLAs

In Jawari, SLA monitoring begins with the selection of benchmarks that are able to collect information about the assessed SLAs and the involved resources. In some situations, multiple benchmarks might be necessary, since they have relationships that help their results analysis. For example, a 3-node Probe is embedded in a Gather Probe, as well as the Long Pipe is a kind of Mixed Bag. Basically all benchmarks contain a Single Connection, and most of them, a Single Task too. Therefore, collective benchmark results permit parallel assessments that can point out some QoS variables, that would be difficult to be revealed in isolation.

The next step is to choose their frequency of execution. They can be scheduled to be executed either at random times within a time window, or at specific moments (some days of the week, some hours of the day, during a period of time, etc). Some aspects must be considered at this point, namely the acceptable SLA violation detection latency and the overhead the target services are able to handle without compromising SLA fulfillment. This decision depends on the characteristics of each system, and on the complexity of the benchmarks. A good way to mitigate the problem would be the creation of independent schedules with distinct frequencies for different groups of benchmarks and resources.

Finally, the user needs to specify SLA violation conditions as events. They are specified independently from the benchmarks schedules. So, when creating a new schedule, the user can select which ones will be tested during and after each benchmark execution, and which actions (notifications) will be performed in case their conditions are satisfied. This enables not only to fix problems that have caused SLA violations, but also treat threats before they become a real violations.

Each event contains a logical expression that adopts a Java like syntax. It supports all Java arithmetic, relational and logical operators [17]. Additionally, it supports the relational operator *matches* that tests if a text string matches a regular expression, as shown in Expression 4.

Besides constant numbers and text strings, benchmark properties and statistical functions can also be used as operands. Benchmark properties follow the pattern shown in Expression 1, with the benchmark name written without spaces, followed by a property name. Table 1 lists the properties used in the following examples. For a complete list of properties, please visit: *jawari.net/help*.

Table 1.   Benchmark properties

Property	Description
value	latest result in the proper measurement unit
success	latest percentage of successful executions (on different resources)
errorMessage	text string with the latest error messages (empty if none)
values(n)	collection of the past n results
successes(n)	collection of the past n success rates

Some properties like *values(n)* and *successes(n)* return collections of values. They are used as arguments for statistical functions, namely $avg()$ (arithmetic mean), $median()$, $max()$ (maximum value), $min()$ (minimum value), $stddev()$ (standard deviation) and $mad()$ (median absolute deviation).

This mechanism permits a variety of possibilities for controlling the grid services adherence to SLAs. The event of Expression 1 tests if a service is still up and running, but not operational. If so, the notification could be the execution of a remote script to restart the Job Manager.

$$SingleConnection.value == 1 \; \&\& \; StaticSingleTask.success == 0 \qquad (1)$$

The example shown in Expression 2 checks if the availability of the benchmarked service was lower than 80%, during the past 30 days. If so, the notification could be an email sent to a system administrator alerting of the SLA violation.

$$avg(SingleConnection.values(30)) < 0.80 \qquad (2)$$

The Expression 3 checks if the job turnaround time of a Dynamic Single Task is at least 10% higher than the median of the times registered by historical executions of the same benchmark.

$$DynamicSingleTask.value > median(DynamicSingleTask.values()) * 1.10 \qquad (3)$$

The event of Expression 4 tests if the user is unauthorized to use a resource. The notification could be an email sent to a VO administrator.

$$StaticSingleTask.errorMessage \ \ matches \ \ ". * User \backslash snot \backslash sauthorized. * " \qquad (4)$$

Events can also be based on custom benchmarks. Considering a user specified benchmark named Whetstone that performs a series of floating-point operations, the event shown in Expression 5 tests if the performance of the benchmarked resource has ever been lower than 300 Mflop/s.

$$min(Whetstone.values()) < 300 \qquad (5)$$

Ultimately, Jawari allows real applications to be specified as custom benchmarks for further execution with all the SLA monitoring support.

6. Conclusion

In this paper we presented a multi-platform and extensible grid benchmarking service that provides the grid community with an instrumental tool for SLA assessment, monitoring and enforcement in grid environments.

We intend to enrich the tool with more benchmarks, more statistical functions and a mechanism capable of deriving the event conditionals from high level SLA statements, in order to simplify SLA monitoring configuration. We also intend to develop a QoS prediction tool, responsible for analyzing historical results in the Repository and correlating parameters such as middleware system, VO, execution time, site and resources with levels of QoS likely to be observed in similar circumstances. This tool would improve the event notification mechanism and consequently the SLA monitoring possibilities.

Jawari is part of the D-Grid initiative [16], and has been in production since November 2006. Among the users are system administrators from several institutions, including the Leibniz Supercomputing Center (LRZ), the University of Dortmund and the Karlsruhe Institute of Technology (KIT). Jawari benchmarks have also allowed software developers and support teams from the OurGrid and gLite communities to automatize tests and identify bugs in new releases of their respective middleware systems. Additionally, it is being used as an information provider for the scheduling algorithm employed by the MediGrid application [10], and we are currently working on MDS aggregators to make Jawari results accessible through the D-Mon Monitoring Service [18].

We encourage users to contribute to the project becoming independent developers. They have been fundamental for the project, making comments and suggestions of improvement and implementing new features. More information can be obtained at the web site: *jawari.net.*

References

[1] E. Oliveira. Jawari - A Grid Benchmarking Service. German E-Science Conference, May 2007.

[2] G. Chun, H. Dail, H. Casanova, and A. Snavely. Benchmark Probes for Grid Assessment. Technical report, University of California, 2003.

[3] Bal, H. et al. Next Generation Grids 2: Requirements and Options for European Grids - Research 2005-2010 and Beyond, 2004. URL: ftp://ftp.cordis.europa.eu/pub/ist/docs/ngg2_eg_final.pdf.

[4] M. Frumkin and R. F. V. Wijngaart. NAS Grid Benchmarks: A Tool for Grid Space Exploration. In Proceedings of the 10th IEEE International Symposium on High Performance Distributed Computing, 2001.

[5] A. Hoheisel and U. Der. An XML-based Framework for Loosely Coupled Applications on Grid Environments. Technical report, Fraunhofer FIRST, Berlin, 2003.

[6] M. Hovestadt. Operation of an SLA-aware Grid Fabric. Journal of Computer Science, 2(6):550–557. 2006

[7] R. A. Kaizar, R. J. Al-ali, K. Amin, G. V. Laszewski, O. F. Rana, D. W. Walker, M. Hategan, and N. Zaluzec. Analysis and Provision of QoS for Distributed Grid Applications. Journal of Grid Computing, 2:163–182, 2004.

[8] C. Ragusa, F. Longo, and A. Puliafito. On the Assessment of the S-Sicilia Infrastructure: A Grid-Based Business System. Grid Economics and Business Models (GECON 2008), In Proceedings of the 5th International Workshop, pages 113–124, August 26, 2008.

[9] A. Sahai, S. Graupner, V. Machiraju, and A. Moorsel. Specifying and Monitoring Guarantees in Commercial Grids through SLA. In Proceedings of the 3rd IEEE/ACM CCGrid, 2003.

[10] D. Sommerfeld, and H. Richter. A Novel Approach to Workflow Scheduling in MediGRID. Technical report, Institut für Informatik, Technische Universität Clausthal, July 2009.

[11] W. Cirne, F. Brasileiro, J. Sauve, N. Andrade, D. Paranhos, E. Santos-Neto and R. Medeiros. Grid Computing for Bag of Tasks Applications. In Proceedings of the 3rd IFIP Conference on E-Commerce, E-Business and E-Government, 2003.

[12] M. Rambadt and Ph. Wieder. UNICORE - Globus Interoperability: Getting the Best of Both Worlds. In Proceedings of the 11th International Symposium on High Performance Distributed Computing (HPDC), Edinburgh, Scotland, IEEE Computer Society Press, page 422, 2002.

[13] gLite Middleware. http://glite.web.cern.ch/glite.

[14] Globus Toolkit. http://www.globus.org.

[15] Unicore - Uniform Interface to Computing Resources. http://unicore.eu.

[16] D-Grid Initiative. http://www.d-grid.de.

[17] Java. Sun Microsystems. http://java.sun.com.

[18] D-MON: D-Grid Monitoring Service. http://www.d-grid.de/index.php?id=41.

[19] Linpack Benchmarks. http://www.netlib.org/linpack.

[20] Nagios Monitoring System. http://www.nagios.org.

REACTIVE MONITORING OF SERVICE LEVEL AGREEMENTS

Dalia Khader, Julian Padget
Department of Computer Science
University of Bath, United Kingdom
ddk20@bath.ac.uk
jap@bath.ac.uk

Martijn Warnier
Systems Engineering
Faculty of Technology, Policy and Management
Delft University of Technology
The Netherlands
m.e.warnier@tudelft.nl

Abstract   Service Level Agreements require a monitoring system that checks that no party violates the agreement. Current monitoring techniques either have a high performance overhead or are not reliable enough. This paper proposes a new hybrid monitoring system that we call *reactive monitoring*. It tries to balance the disadvantages of established monitoring techniques, in particular online and offline monitoring. Online monitoring has a relatively high performance overhead and offline monitoring does not identify all possible violations.

Reactive monitoring combines online monitoring, which is used for reactively checking continuous SLA properties with a new *passive monitoring scheme*. This scheme is used for monitoring discrete SLA properties. It is based on cryptographic primitives that provide proof that either a certain stage in an interaction has been reached correctly with all participants in compliance of the service level agreements or that a violation has occurred. In the latter case the violating party can be identified.

A theoretical analysis shows that in the worst case scenario this new approach has the same overhead as online monitoring techniques and in most cases the overhead will be significantly lower.

Keywords: Service Level Agreements, Reactive Monitoring, Passive Monitoring, Multi Party Contract Signing Protocol, Aggregate Signatures, Violations

P. Wieder et al. (eds.), *Grids and Service-Oriented Architectures for Service Level Agreements,*
DOI 10.1007/978-1-4419-7320-7_2, © Springer Science+Business Media, LLC 2010

1.   Introduction

Service Level Agreements (SLAs) form an essential part of distributed computing, in particular in environments such as grid, cloud and service oriented computing. A SLA represents an agreement between a client and a provider in the context of a particular service provision. SLAs can be between two (one-to-one) or more (one-to-many, or many-to-many) parties. A SLA typically consists of a number of Service Level Objectives (SLOs) that define Quality of Service (QoS) properties for the agreed upon service. The preceding negotiation and agreement of SLAs are outside the scope of this paper, but see for example [9, 14]for more on these subjects. These QoS properties need to be measurable and must be monitored during the provision of the service that has been agreed in the SLA.

Typically, an independent trusted third party (TTP) is used to monitor the agreement. Two approaches can be distinguished for monitoring SLAs. The first type is *online* monitoring [10–12]. This involves periodically testing whether the agreement terms have been met by all relevant parties. The monitoring interval can vary, depending on the agreement's SLOs, but in general it has to be quite small (of the order of seconds). A property such as network bandwidth, for example, has to be monitored continuously if one wants to ensure that the SLO is not violated. The other approach is *offline* monitoring. In this case all interactions are recorded, typically at the client site [6], and securely logged and stored by the monitor [4]. If a party to the agreed upon SLA thinks that the terms have been violated, the log is examined to establish whether a violation took place.

Both types of monitoring come at a cost. Online monitoring is hard to implement in an efficient way. It has a relatively high performance overhead and the monitoring system typically forms a bottleneck since all parties in all interactions contact it throughout. The disadvantage of offline monitoring is the need for storage and, more importantly, this type of monitoring cannot always prove with certainty that a violation has taken place[11]. If, for example, the network bandwidth at the client site drops, did this happen because the provider violated the SLA or because the client is under a denial of service attack? Some research, most notably by Jurca et. al. [10] has tried to extend monitoring with reputation based mechanisms in order to fix this problem. But reputation mechanisms have their own reliability problems [7].

This paper proposes a new monitoring technique that tries to balance the trade-offs of the monitoring approaches discussed above. In the worst case scenario the new hybrid approach has the same overhead as online monitoring techniques and in most cases the overhead will be significantly lower. The new technique depends on what we refer to as *passive monitoring*. Passive monitoring is an offline monitoring scheme that uses cryptographic primitives to provide proof that a certain stage of an interaction has been reached correctly, i.e., without any of the parties violating the SLA. The proofs are exchanged between the communicating parties without the help of a trusted third party. The proposed *reactive monitoring scheme* is a hybrid approach to monitoring. It combines online monitoring with the new (offline) *passive monitoring scheme.* In the case that a dispute arises an (online) monitor is contacted. At this point the parties either prove they have reached that stage correctly, in full compliance with the SLA, by providing the most recent cryptographic primitive they have. Or, alternatively, one of the parties is in violation, which can be proved from the cryptographic primitive they present. The protocol used in exchanging these primitives is called the service evidential protocol (SEP). In the case that no violation was proven the parties have the option to renegotiate their monitoring policy. At this point they can agree to use online monitoring for some fixed time period before switching back to the passive monitoring scheme.

2. Preliminaries

This section describes two preliminaries used as building blocks for the passive monitoring scheme.

2.1 Contract Signing Protocols

A contract signing protocol (CSP) is a cryptographic protocol that allows two or more parties to exchange signatures on a contract such that no party receives a signed contract unless all of them do, achieving what literature refers to as fairness, as first proposed by Even [2]. The obvious solution to implement such a protocol is to utilize a trusted third party (TTP) that collects a digitally signed contract from all participants and redistributes or aborts. However, this solution is not ideal since the TTP becomes a performance bottleneck. Two solutions have been proposed in the literature in order to address this problem. The first is to eliminate the involvement of the TTP [3], where the general idea is to exchange signatures gradually. However, these solutions are nondeterministic, which in most cases would be a problem for the signatories and is expensive in terms of computation and communication. A second solution is to construct a CSP while minimizing interaction with the TTP. An optimistic protocol only depends on the TTP when there is a dispute. In other words the TTP is never contacted if all signing parties are behaving in compliance with the protocol [4, 13]. For this paper we assume the usage of a CSP to finalize a service level agreement and to support SEP. We leave the decision of which type of CSP to use for future studies, but there are several candidates in the literature [4, 8].

In the remainder of this paper we will not distinguish between a trusted third party and a monitor. All monitors are trusted third parties, for the sake of readability we only speak of monitors in the sequel.

2.2   Aggregate Signatures

An aggregate signature is a digital signature scheme that supports aggregation [1] and is one of the main building blocks for a SEP. Given n signatures for n distinct messages from n different users, it is possible to merge them into one single signature. The following are the algorithms:

- Setup: Each user i has a public key pk_i and a secret key sk_i.
- Sign: Using the message M and secret key sk_i as input create a signature $\sigma_i = S(M, sk_i)$
- Verify: Using the public key pk_i, the message M and the signature σ_i as input verify a signature σ_i. $V(\sigma_i, M, pk_i) = \{accept, reject\}$. This tells us whether σ_i was in fact created by user i.
- Aggregate Signature: Having signature $\sigma_1, ..., \sigma_n$ as inputs create one short signature. $\sigma = A(\sigma_1, ..., \sigma_n)$.
- Verify Aggregation: Having several public keys $pk_1, ..., pk_n$, several messages $M_1, ..., M_n$ and one aggregation σ verify the aggregation: $R(\sigma, pk_1, ..., pk_n, M_1, ..., M_n) = \{accept, reject\}$. Which tells us if all signatures been created by their corresponding users.

3.   Service Evidential Protocol

The service evidential protocol (SEP) is a protocol that allows for the collection of evidence of SLA compliant behavior of the communicating parties over the period of their interaction. The general idea is to minimize the usage of the monitoring system for SLA agreement. We start from a presumption of good intentions by all parties to the SLA. However, if at any point one of the parties suspects any of the other parties of non-compliance, it calls on the monitor who is, by definition, trusted by all. At this point one of two situations can occur: (i) one of the parties is in violation of the SLA. The monitor identifies the violating party by inspecting the cryptographic signatures, aborts the service and penalizes the offender. Appropriate penalties can be negotiated and be part of the SLA [11]. Or, (ii) all parties are in compliance with the SLA and can prove this by presenting the appropriate cryptographic signatures. In this case, the parties can either renegotiate a new, possibly online, monitoring scheme or can continue using passive monitoring.

So in the most optimistic outcome the monitor never gets involved. If a dispute occurs, the violating party can be identified and penalized. In addition, the parties can renegotiate the monitoring policy and revert to conventional monitoring (i.e., offline or online depending on the service and SLA). This can be done easily as long as the service provided is discrete and state based. Continuous QoS-like properties cannot be monitored in this manner. In Section 5 we discuss how passive and online monitoring can be combined in a hybrid approach, reactive monitoring, that can monitor both discrete and continuous properties.

The general idea of the protocol is as follows:

1. The service provider starts by sending the service encrypted with the *monitor's* public key to the client
2. The response of the client is a signature on the received ciphertext
3. On receiving the signed ciphertext, the service provider responds with an encrypted service to the client

The client can verify that the receipt he has given out was on the service he requested and the service provider has a signature of the client that provides non-repudiation: the client cannot deny ordering the service.

We adopt the standard naming convention in the cryptographic literature and refer to the service provider as Alice and the service client as Bob.

Consider the following example:

SCENARIO 1 *Alice provides memory storage. Bob is interested in using Alice's service for a week. Alice and Bob sign a contract that states the SLA. The contract indicates that to obtain memory storage Bob will need a password that expires every day. The states of the interaction can be divided to seven stages in which Bob asks every day for a new password from Alice. In the SLA agreement both parties agreed on hiring Matilda as a passive monitor.*

One can assume that the password is the service provided, and we notate it as M to Bob. Alice has the key pair (pk_a, sk_a), Bob has (pk_b, sk_b), and Matilda has (pk_m, sk_m). We refer to the encryption algorithm as E, the decryption algorithm as D and the signing algorithm as S throughout the paper. The steps are as follows:

1. Alice sends Bob the ciphertext $C_1 = E(M, pk_m)$ and $\sigma_a = S(C_1, sk_a)$. If Bob does not respond then Alice has not revealed any information because the service is encrypted with Matilda's key.
2.a Bob verifies σ_a then replies with sending Alice $\sigma_b = S(C_1, sk_b)$. σ_b represents a receipt in the context of SEP (success).
2.b If Bob does not get a reply (σ_a), he can contact Matilda and she can recover the service M (from the previous step). Matilda will at this point give Bob the encrypted service $C_2 = E(M, pk_b)$, which she can construct from message C_1. If Matilda establishes that M is not the service agreed upon in the CSP, she signs an abort message to Bob and the algorithm halts (fail).
3. Alice on receiving the receipt σ_b can verify it and send Bob the encrypted service $C_2 = E(M, pk_b)$.

Figure 1 is a diagram presenting the above protocol.

Alice	Bob
$C_1 = E(M, pk_m)$	
$\sigma_a = S(C_1, sk_a)$	

$\xrightarrow{\quad C_1, \sigma_a \quad}$

$$V(\sigma_a, C_1, pk_a) = \{accept, reject\}$$
$$\sigma_b = S(C_1, sk_b)$$

$\xleftarrow{\quad \sigma_b \quad}$

$$V(\sigma_b, C_1, pk_b) = \{accept, reject\}$$
$$C_2 = E(M, pk_b)$$

$\xrightarrow{\quad C_2 \quad}$

$$D(C_2, sk_b) = M$$

Figure 1. Optimistic Approach - No monitor needed

4.   Passive Monitoring Scheme

If two or more parties to a SLA decide to use a passive monitoring scheme (PMS), they should specify the monitoring party to use in case of dispute. Once the negotiation ends a contract signing protocol takes place. This serves to finalize the agreement and helps identify violating parties in case of disputes.

We assume that the service level agreement is a set of states that occur one after another. For example, if we are talking about memory storage as the type of service, a state would be the amount of memory reserved for a certain party over a certain time period. Each time the interaction reaches a new state the parties run SEP and exchange receipts. Each entity aggregates the new receipt with the old ones. If a dispute arises the monitor asks all parties to provide the latest aggregated signature they have calculated and the latest encrypted service.

The aggregate signature will refer to the state the party has reached. If all parties have reached the same state then the monitor concludes that all parties are acting in compliance with the SLA and decrypt the ciphertexts received and distribute them. The monitoring can then continue in passive manner. Figure 1 presents the interaction between Alice and Bob when the monitor Matilda is not contacted while Figure 2 demonstrates the interactions in case the monitor is needed. Note that A_a is the aggregation by Alice throughout the interaction, A_b is the signature aggregation by Bob during the interaction and $Chk(CSP)$ refers to checking the contract signing protocol to see what services should have been provided at each state of the interaction.

Examining Figure 2 in detail, we see that Bob claims he has sent a receipt to Alice but has not got the service he requested. He sends Matilda the ciphertext and signature he got from Alice (C_1, σ_a). Furthermore, he sends Matilda an aggregate signature of his A_b indicating the state he has reached with Alice in the interaction. He also sends a receipt copy σ_b to Matilda as proof of

Alice	Matilda	Bob
		$\xleftarrow{C_1, \sigma_a, A_b, \sigma_b}$
$\xrightarrow{A_a}$		
$\xleftarrow{abort, Penalize}$	if$(V(\sigma_a, C_1, pk_a) = reject$	$\xrightarrow{abort}$
	Else	
	$D(C_1, sk_m) = \bar{M}$	
$\xleftarrow{abort, Penalize}$	$Chk(CSP)$ and if $(\bar{M} \neq M)$	$\xrightarrow{abort}$
	Else	
$\xleftarrow{abort, Penalize}$	$Chk(CSP)$ and if $(R(A_a, pk_1, ..., pk_n, M_1, ..., M_n) = reject)$	$\xrightarrow{abort}$
	Else	
$\xleftarrow{abort}$	$Chk(CSP)$ and if $(R(A_b, pk_1, ..., pk_n, M_1, ..., M_n) = reject)$	$\xrightarrow{abort, Penalize}$
	Else	
$\xleftarrow{abort}$	if $(V(\sigma_b, C_1, pk_b))$	$\xrightarrow{abort, Penalize}$
	Else	
$\xleftarrow{\sigma_b}$	$E(M, pk_b) = C_2$	$\xrightarrow{C_2}$
$V(\sigma_b, C_1, pk_b) = \{accept, reject\}$		$D(C_2, sk_b) = M$

Figure 2. Monitor mediation required

good intention. Matilda asks Alice to provide her with an aggregate signature too. Matilda can verify the signatures she got from both parties and decrypt the message she got from Bob. She compares the service M, the state of interaction, i.e., comparing aggregate signatures, and the receipts with the SLA contract. If everything seems compatible with the contract, Matilda can assume an unreliable connection between Alice and Bob. She then forwards the service encrypted to Bob and Bob's receipt is sent to Alice.

The proposed passive monitoring scheme uses asymmetric (public key) encryption for all operations. This is expensive and not necessary. A typical optimization would be to use public key encryption to establish the receipts together with a session key and then use this key with a (cheaper) *symmetric* encryption scheme or the actual (encrypted) service.

5. Reactive Monitoring Scheme

The passive monitoring scheme introduced in the previous section is not able to monitor continuous QoS-like properties such as network bandwidth or processing power. Additionally, we observe that some QoS properties, in particular security, are very hard to monitor. None of the existing monitoring techniques, including passive or reactive monitoring, is capable of dealing with these. However, for continuous properties we propose a *reactive* approach. At the moment that one of the parties to an SLA suspects that a continuous property is violated it can contact an online monitor. Using continuous monitoring it tries to establish if a violation has taken place. Since the offending party will not be notified until after the inspection is performed, there is a reasonable probability of detecting most violations in this way. Figure 3 illustrates the complete reactive monitoring scheme.

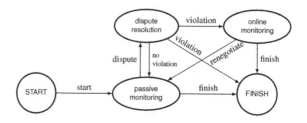

Figure 3.   State diagram of reactive monitoring scheme

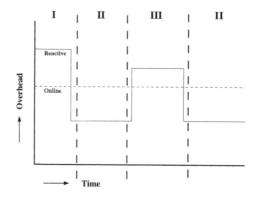

Figure 4.   Expected overhead of online and reactive monitoring

The reactive monitoring scheme proposed in this paper tries to balance the disadvantages of both online and offline monitoring. The advantage with respect to offline monitoring should be clear: in contrast to offline monitoring, reactive monitoring detects all occurrences of violations and can always identify the offending party.

The advantage with regards to online monitoring is perhaps less clear. At first glance reactive monitoring seems to be more expensive since it uses some expensive cryptographic operations and also uses online monitoring as a sub-part of its process. However, we argue that *on average* reactive monitoring has a smaller performance overhead compared to online monitoring. Figure 4 displays a hypothetical view of the expected overhead over the time period of a typical SLA. However, we have not represented offline monitoring costs on the graph, because it is not clear to us to where to attribute the costs or how large they should be at different times.

Three different phases can be distinguished:

- Phase **I**: This is the initialization phase of the reactive monitoring scheme. Several cryptographic operations have to be performed to use the passive monitoring scheme, and its overhead will thus be higher than online monitoring at this stage.

- **Phase II**: Under normal circumstances online monitoring will on average be more expensive than reactive monitoring. The reactive monitoring scheme does not continuously inspect the provided service, but will only occasionally forward and sign some service requests.

- **Phase III**: If a (possible) violation is signalled by one of the parties the monitor either (i) checks the credentials, for discrete SLA properties, to determine if a violation has occurred and to identify the offending party (if any), or (ii) an online monitor is used to determine retrospectively if a continuous property has been violated. In this phase the reactive monitoring scheme will again be more expensive than online monitoring.

We argue that on average phase **II** will be much more common then either phase **I** or **III**. This will in particular be the case if the number of violations is relatively low. From this we conclude that, when measured over a longer time period, the cumulative cost of reactive monitoring will be lower than the costs of online monitoring.

Obviously, this argument is only a first step towards a full analysis of the difference in performance overhead between reactive and online monitoring. For one thing, we have not defined what overhead exactly means: number of used messages, cpu or memory usage or something else? We do believe that reactive monitoring can be beneficial under typical situations and deserves further research. Our next step is to implement the passive monitoring scheme and compare its performance (overhead) with other approaches in different circumstances, possibly using some of the ALIVE (see http://www.ist-alive.eu) scenarios as testbeds.

In summary, the reactive monitoring scheme is a hybrid approach that combines passive monitoring, as introduced in Section 4, with online monitoring. This combination should provide reliable monitoring with an overhead that is smaller than with conventional online monitoring.

6.   Conclusions

This paper introduces *reactive monitoring*: a monitoring paradigm that combines classical online monitoring with a new passive monitoring scheme based on aggregate contract signing protocols. A theoretical analysis of the new monitoring scheme shows that in typical circumstances reactive monitoring has a lower overhead than online monitoring. The next step is to implement the reactive monitoring scheme and show through empirical experiments that the overhead is indeed lower.

Acknowledgments

This work is partially supported through the ALIVE project (FP7-IST-215890)

References

[1] D. Boneh, B. Lynn, and H. Shacham. Short signatures from the weil pairing. Journal of Cryptology, 17(4):297–319, 2004.

[2] S. Even. Protocol for signing contracts. In CRYPTO'81, pages 148–153, 1981.

[3] S. Even, O. Goldreich, and A. Lempel. A randomized protocol for signing contracts. Commun. ACM, 28(6):637–647, 1985.

[4] J. Garay, M. Jakobsson, and P. MacKenzie. Abuse-free optimistic contract signing. In CRYPTO'99, LNCS, Vol. 1666, page 787, Springer, 1999.

[5] L. Gymnopoulos, S. Dritsas, S. Gritzalis, and C. Lambrinoudakis. GRID security review. LNCS, pages 100–111, 2003.

[6] R. Jurca, B. Faltings, and W. Binder. Reliable QoS monitoring based on client feedback. In Proceedings of the 16th international conference on World Wide Web, pages 1003–1012, ACM Press New York, NY, USA, 2007.

[7] R. Kerr and R. Cohen. Smart cheaters do prosper: Defeating trust and reputation systems. In Proceedings of the Eigth International Conference on Autonomous Agents and Multi-Agent Systems, 2009.

[8] A. Mukhamedov and M. Ryan. Improved multi-party contract signing. In Financial Cryptography and Data Security, LNCS, Vol. 4886, pages 179–191, Springer, 2007.

[9] A. Pichot, P. Wieder, O. Wäldrich, and W. Ziegler. Dynamic SLA-negotiation based on WS-Agreement. Technical Report TR-0082, Institute on Resource Management and Scheduling, CoreGRID - Network of Excellence, June 2007.

[10] F. Raimondi, J. Skene, and W. Emmerich. Efficient online monitoring of web-service SLAs. In SIGSOFT '08/FSE-16: Proceedings of the 16th ACM SIGSOFT International Symposium on Foundations of software engineering, pages 170–180, New York, USA, 2008.

[11] O. Rana, M. Warnier, T. B. Quillinan, and F. M. T. Brazier Monitoring and Reputation Mechanisms for Service Level Agreements. In Proceedings of the 5th International Workshop on Grid Economics and Business Models (GenCon), Las Palmas, Gran Canaria, Spain, Springer, August 2008.

[12] A. Sahai, S. Graupner, V. Machiraju, and A. van Moorsel. Specifying and monitoring guarantees in commercial grids through SLA. In Proceedings of the 3rd IEEE/ACM International Symposium on Cluster Computing and the Grid, pages 292–299, 2003.

[13] B. Waidner and M. Waidner. Round-optimal and abuse-free optimistic multi-party contract signing. In Automata Languages and Programming, LNCS, Vol. 1853, pages 524–535, Springer, 2000.

[14] W. Ziegler, P. Wieder, and D. Battre. Extending WS-Agreement for dynamic negotiation of Service Level Agreements. Technical Report TR-0172, Institute on Resource Management and Scheduling, CoreGRID - Network of Excellence, August 2008.

LESSONS LEARNED FROM IMPLEMENTING WS-AGREEMENT

Dominic Battré, Matthias Hovestadt
Technische Universität Berlin, Germany
{dominic.battre, matthias.hovestadt}@tu-berlin.de

Oliver Wäldrich
Department of Bioinformatics
Fraunhofer Institute SCAI
53754 Sankt Augustin, Germany
oliver.waeldrich@scai.fraunhofer.de

Abstract   WS-Agreement describes a protocol and structure for creating and representing service level agreements. In order to remain domain independent, the authors of the WS-Agreement specification have provided many extension points for domain specific content. This creates high degrees of freedoms for programmers to implement the specification. Many attempts to do this have been made in the past. In this paper, we explain what we have learned from our own and other projects' attempts of implementing WS-Agreement. The paper presents a set of guidelines how the features of WS-Agreement can be used in a sound way that allows transferring large parts of the WS-Agreement logic into a generic and domain-independent WS-Agreement framework.

Keywords: WS-Agreement, Modeling, Best Practices, Agreement Templates, Automatic Evaluation

P. Wieder et al. (eds.), *Grids and Service-Oriented Architectures for Service Level Agreements,*
DOI 10.1007/978-1-4419-7320-7_3, © Springer Science+Business Media, LLC 2010

1. Introduction

The WS-Agreement specification [1] of the GRAAP-WG (Grid Resource Allocation Agreement Protocol Working Group) of the Open Grid Forum (OGF) is a protocol that allows two parties to express and close electronic contracts. In order to achieve this, WS-Agreement provides an XML Schema definition that allows describing the content of Service Level Agreements (SLAs) and a protocol with message definitions that can be used to agree on contracts. The XML Schema provides information about the basic structure of agreements but intentionally does not address the concrete and domain specific description of the terms that parties want to agree upon. These so called term languages need to be contributed by additional XML Schema definitions.

Several projects have (partially) implemented the WS-Agreement specification during the recent years since it has become an OGF proposed recommendation. By inspecting the outcomes of these projects and also of our own attempts to implement WS-Agreement[1], we have discovered that most projects use only a fraction of WS-Agreement. Our hypothesis is that this results from the problem that WS-Agreement does not provide sufficient instructional information on how to use it. Through the recent years we have found several non-obvious ways to exploit WS-Agreement and to allow large parts of its logic to be shifted into domain-independent frameworks, which significantly simplifies the use of WS-Agreement for a specific application. Herein, we want to provide our conclusions in the form of a set of best practices on how to use WS-Agreement.

The remainder of this paper is structured as follows: First, related work on WS-Agreement is presented in section 2. Section 3 addresses the protocol used to create agreements, and the structure of these agreements is then discussed in section 4. Section 5 addresses agreement templates before section 7 concludes the paper.

2. Related work

Early work on Service Level Agreements in the scope of Web Services and Grid computing has been published Ludwig et al. in [2]. Their work culminated in the WS-Agreement specification [1], which is currently a proposed recommendation by the Open Grid Forum. Wieder et al. present in [3] a survey of various WS-Agreement implementations, though at a rather conceptual level. More technical details on attempts to implement WS-Agreement can be found in papers by Hasselmeyer et al. [4] and Battré et al. [5]. The question of modeling

---

[1]The use of WS-Agreement in AgentScape, AssessGrid, BEinGRID Experiments 20, 22, and 25, BREIN, JSS, and Phosphorus has been considered. Details can be found in an upcoming experience document of WS-Agreement in the scope of the Open Grid Forum.

SLAs with WS-Agreement has been discussed for example by Rana et al. [6] and Battré et al. [7].

3.   Protocol

Agreements that follow the WS-Agreement specification are always instantiated between exactly two parties. These two parties take the roles of Agreement Initiator and Agreement Responder. WS-Agreement does not prescribe which role is taken by a customer and which role is taken by a provider. In most projects investigated, however, the customer takes the role of the Agreement Initiator.

The agreement creation process follows a very simple two step protocol: First, the Agreement Initiator submits an agreement offer to the Agreement Responder. Then the Agreement Responder makes an atomic decision whether to accept this offer or to reject it and notifies the Agreement Initiator of its decision. After this, an Agreement is either established or declined with an exception. The Agreement Responder may not modify the agreement offer in any way.

Two important aspects from this protocol are worth mentioning because they contradict common expectations of an agreement protocol:

- The agreement creation protocol is very simple consisting of just two messages. After the Agreement Initiator has submitted its offer, it is legally bound to this offer in case the Agreement Responder accepts it. We have seen a frequent desire to either invert the order of commitment (i. e. the desire that the offer sent by the Agreement Initiator is non-binding, that it results in a counter-offer by the Agreement Responder to which the latter is bound, and that the Agreement Initiator can commit on this counter-offer) or to at least ask for non-binding offers, called "invitations to treat", where the Agreement Responder replies with a counter-offer that it is generally willing to accept without asserting that it maintains this willingness for any period of time. Neither of this is supported by WS-Agreement as of now! The desire to invert the order of commitment is motivated by various scenarios where for example the provider needs to calculate the price before creating an agreement or where co-allocation of several services is important. WS-Agreement extensions that allow asking for invitations to treat are being developed by the GRAAP working group. We suggest that, in order to circumvent the problem of co-allocation, these mechanisms may be combined with policies that allow a customer to create agreements but terminate those for a small penalty within the first few seconds after their creation in order to perform a roll-back.

- It seems desirable to negotiate an agreement by means of (several) rounds of offers and counter-offers and to modify an accepted agreement at runtime. Neither is supported by WS-Agreement as of now.

4. Structure of Agreements

The content of agreements expressed by means of WS-Agreement, i. e. terms that express what is agreed upon, has been left open to support various domains. The overall structure, however, is common amongst all agreements. It comprises the context of agreements, mainly specifying the two parties involved, and a set of guarantees for expressing what is guaranteed and what penalties and rewards are given in case of violations or compliance. These two static parts are followed by a set of agreement states that expose the runtime state of an agreement. All this information is exposed as WS-Resource Properties and can be summarized in a resource property document. The appendix of this paper contains a sample SLA that explains and illustrates several of the best practices discussed in the following.

4.1 Context

The Agreement Context (lines 4–13 of the sample SLA) comprises a definition of the parties involved in the agreement as well as metadata such as the agreement duration. Furthermore, it provides an extension point for domain specific meta data. We address here only the parties involved in the agreement.

WS-Agreement does not prescribe how the participating parties are identified. The parties could be natural persons (human beings), legal person (e. g. companies, providers, virtual organizations (VO), etc.), but maybe also concrete computing systems. Identity management is a broad topic of ongoing research but for practical purposes we would recommend to just use distinguished names as they are common in secure web service contexts. WS-Agreement does not specify the use of signatures in agreements, but provides for example in the agreement context freedom to add them.

4.2 Terms and States

The Agreement Terms make up the core of an agreement stating what is guaranteed and what happens in case guarantees are adhered to or violated.

WS-Agreement provides two types of terms, Service Description Terms and Guarantee Terms, as well as so called Service References and Service Properties. These elements can be combined by the logical conjunctions "All", "One or More", and "Exactly One" (see lines 16–98).

As it appears generally difficult to work with contracts that contain arbitrarily nested logical conjunctions, we recommend transforming the logical expression of terms into disjunctive normal form before deciding whether an agreement can be fulfilled and therefore accepted. This reduces the task to the simpler problem of deciding whether at least one conjunctive clause can be fulfilled. Most projects investigated did not allow disjunctions of terms.

In the following we will discuss Service Description Terms and their state representation as Service Term States, followed by Service Properties, Guarantee Terms, and Guarantee States.

The aptly named **Service Description Terms** (SDTs) describe the properties of a service offered by the provider (usually Agreement Responder). Lines 18–40 of the sample SLA illustrate this. We recommend the following best practices for Service Description Terms:

- Service Description Terms should reuse structures of well respected specifications such as JSDL for example (or one of its extensions JSDL-POSIX, JSDL-SPMD, etc.) for the sake of interoperability, which is otherwise difficult to achieve. Members of the GRAAP working group of OGF might give useful hints, what has been used in the scope of WS-Agreement in the past.

- The Name attribute of a Service Description Term may carry a semantic meaning that is agreed upon by the programmers developing the client and server side implementations of WS-Agreement. By giving SDTs a name, programmers can anticipate the structure and the meaning of a SDT in the context of an SLA. This simplifies the handling of an SLA on the provider side significantly because service terms can be selected easily by their name and processed by handlers that are registered for the respective SDT names.

- WS-Agreement allows describing different facets of the same service in individual Service Description Terms and linking those together by using the ServiceName attribute of Service Description Terms. This allows separation of concerns and simplifies re-negotiation in the future because individual aspects of an agreement can be referenced and re-negotiated individually.

- For computational services, it is often preferable to describe what will be delivered in terms of services, which encapsulate the logic of one or more programs by a simple interface, than to allow JSDL-POSIX/SPMD like access to the raw compute resources. The reason for this is the sheer number of problems that can occur and make it difficult to decide who has violated his guarantees. In particular a bad exit code of a user submitted program does not indicate whether the input data or the software contains an error, or whether the problem stems from hardware issues or the operating system. By offering the execution of a service, a provider can provide a tested service that performs input file validation and gain more confidence to execute a program successfully. The provider promises a correct result and the reason for incorrect results becomes less important.

Therefore, in the scope of WS-Agreement, Service Grids appear simpler to realize than Compute Grids. Furthermore, they simplify changing providers because file system paths to executables for example are hidden behind the service description.

Each Service Description Term possesses a runtime state (lines 105–124), the so called **Service Term State**. It indicates whether the described aspect of the service is not ready, ready, or completed. The definition of the Service Term State provides an extension point that implementations should use to expose additional runtime or monitoring data for the associated Service Description Term. Even though this is not explicitly suggested by the WS-Agreement specification, our experience showed that this is the most reasonable point to expose this data during SLA execution. Moreover, extensive runtime information is of particular importance for the definition of guarantees and their service level objectives. The example illustrates how this runtime information is included in the Service Term State. Note that the user has requested a *minimum* CPU speed of 2 GHz (line 33) but was given CPUs of 3 GHz clock rate (line 114).

The Service Description Terms do not make any guarantees by themselves. The guarantees and consequences of adherence and violation are formulated in Guarantee Terms. Before addressing those, we need to discuss Service Properties, as they constitute a central tool for guarantee description and evaluation.

Service Properties (line 41–65) allow the definition of variables. A variable consists of an identifier, a metric, and a location expression. If Service Term States expose the actual configuration or monitoring data of service aspects as suggested above, this enables to refer to these values by newly introduced variables as presented in the example. All resource properties of an Agreement are summarized in a resource properties document upon which the location expressions can be evaluated. Note the difficulty of using XPath expressions with namespace prefixes. In order to bind namespace prefixes one can resort for example to using XQuery or one could define static prefix bindings, which means however that the SLA is not self-containing.

Given these variables, it is possible to express guarantees in the form of **Guarantee Terms** using for example the Java Expression Language (JEXL), any other expression language is possible as well, as shown in lines 66–96. A WS-Agreement implementation could then just lookup the variable valuations from the resource properties document and evaluate the JEXL expression using a standard interpreter.

Note how the combination of JEXL expressions with variables can be used to define qualifying conditions for Guarantee Terms as well as for determining whether Guarantee Terms are fulfilled. Likewise they can be used to define Value Expressions for penalties and rewards.

We want to point out two important topics in the context of SLA compliance.

- WS-Agreement does not allow an SLA to be violated. The SLA can be in various states (see chapter 7.1 "Agreement States" of the WS-Agreement specification [1]), but these indicate only position in the life-cycle of the SLA. Only Guarantee Terms can be violated. We have seen a frequent desire to express that an either the entire SLA is fulfilled or violated. This can be modeled by aggregating several conditions into one guarantee as shown in lines 73–78. These lines comprise the conditions that the job starts after the earliest possible start time, terminates before the latest possible finish time, and uses CPUs of at least the specified clock rate. Note how the expression remains correct even if the job termination time is not known, yet.

- Penalties and Rewards carry an assessment interval defining the duration over which a service level objective is observed. If a Service Level Objective (SLO) always evaluates to true during this time, a reward is paid; otherwise a penalty is paid. After that the monitoring continues. It is often desirable that a penalty is paid only once: If an SLO is ever violated, the SLA should be considered violated as well and a penalty shall be paid. This can be modeled by an empty Service Level Objective that is evaluated only once and bears a positive reward. This represents the fee (reward) of the SLA. In addition to that, a compound SLO carries the guarantees and a penalty. In order to express that the penalty is paid only at the first time the SLO is violated, one can for example wrap the content of the Value Expression of the Penalty with a custom <onlyOnce> tag or use a Custom Business Value. Unfortunately, something like this has not been standardized, yet.

The status of guarantees is exposed as **Guarantee States** to the user. Just like the previous states, a user can query these states by means of the WS-Resource Framework and subscribe to them by means of WS-Notification.

5.   Templates

Templates play an important role in WS-Agreement for advertising what kind of services and QoS a provider can offer and for automatically evaluating whether the content filled into a template is valid. Even though often expected, templates *do not* serve the purpose of telling the Agreement Initiator which fields to fill very well but instead describe what the filled out template will look like.

An Agreement Template is an extension of the regular Agreement structure by so called Creation Constraints. A Creation Constraint consists of an XPath or XQuery pointing to elements within the agreement and an XML Schema definition for elements located at these positions. By means of XML Schema validation it is possible to automatically determine whether an Agreement complies with the Creation Constraints. The following example shows how this mechanism may be used to limit requests to ask for only one or two CPUs in each node.

```
<wsag:Item wsag:Name="JobDefinition_JobDescription_Resources_\
IndividualCPUCount_Exact@JOB_DESCRIPTION">

    <wsag:Location>
        declare namespace jsdl='...'; declare namespace wsag='...';
        $this/wsag:AgreementOffer/wsag:Terms/wsag:All/
        wsag:ServiceDescriptionTerm[@wsag:Name='JOB_DESCRIPTION']/
        jsdl:JobDefinition/jsdl:JobDescription/jsdl:Resources/
        jsdl:IndividualCPUCount/jsdl:Exact
    </wsag:Location>

    <wsag:ItemConstraint>
        <xs:minInclusive value="1" xmlns:xs="..."/>
        <xs:maxInclusive value="2" xmlns:xs="..."/>
    </wsag:ItemConstraint>

</wsag:Item>
```

Note how difficult it is to automatically extract the information that this creation constraint limits the number of CPUs in each node. This underlines one of our central claims:

The structure of Agreement Templates needs to be known to Agreement Initiators and Agreement Responders. A programmer could explicitly look up the range of numbers of CPUs by evaluating two XPath expressions on the Agreement Template, present this range to the user in some graphical user interface, and store the entered value at the correct location in the agreement offer. This requires however that the programmer knows the *structure* (not the concrete values) of the Agreement Template in advance. The structure tells where range limits can be found and where concrete values shall be filled in. As each Agreement Template carries an identifier, it is possible to version templates and provide this information. Similarly, the provider needs to know the structure of the Agreement Template and thereby the structure of incoming agreement offers to be certain whether it can fulfill these offers and that a user does not request something impossible. The Creation Constraints are a means to automatically check that only valid options are requested in the agreement offer and that the agreement offer follows a structure that can be interpreted by the provider.

A different approach to customize agreement offers is to use Exactly One statements in the Agreement Template and ask the user to pick one option and replace the Exactly One statement by this option. This modifies the Agreement structure however. Therefore, it is even more important to guard this by suitable Creation Constraints.

6. Conclusion

WS-Agreement describes a protocol and structure to create and describe service level agreements. In order to remain domain independent, the authors of WS-Agreement have provided many extension points for domain specific parts. Therefore, it is possible to make use of WS-Agreement in a virtually infinite number of different ways. Investigations of various WS-Agreement implementations have shown that many projects make use of only small portions of WS-Agreement and large portions seem to be not well understood.

In this paper we have presented the hypothesis that both parties involved in a WS-Agreement need to know the structure and meaning of a concrete Agreement Template before writing software that requests the creation of agreements and software that instantiates the service described by agreements that are based on this template. Therefore, the created agreements necessarily follow a fairly rigid structure described in the Agreement Template.

If Agreement Templates are designed according to the design guidelines presented in this paper, it becomes possible to

- automatically check whether an agreement offer is valid (by checking Creations Constraints),
- extract limits from the creation constraints and present them in a GUI for the Agreement Initiator (by making use of named Agreement Templates and named Creation Constraints with known structure),
- automatically evaluate the fulfillment and violation of guarantees and bill the parties for this (by valuating variables and evaluating guarantees).

These features can be implemented in a generic WS-Agreement engine and do not need to be considered by a programmer implementing SLAs for a specific domain. This shifts the focus to designing SLA templates. Besides that, the remaining task of the programmer is to

- instantiate services according to the agreement (rather simple due to the known structure of the agreement) and
- expose the actual properties of the agreement as WS-Resource Properties.

Example SLA

```
<wsag:AgreementProperties {namespace declarations}>
  <wsag:Name>Weather Forecast Agreement, 2009-07-19</wsag:Name>
  <wsag:AgreementId>8689d4f3-ae17-4234-bdbd-b814e7c7d6c6</wsag:AgreementId>
  <wsag:Context>
    <wsag:AgreementInitiator xsi:type="ns:DistinguishedName_Type">
      /C=DE/O=GridGermany/OU=TU Berlin/OU=CIT/CN=Dominic Battre
    </wsag:AgreementInitiator>
    <wsag:AgreementResponder>...</wsag:AgreementResponder>
    <wsag:ServiceProvider>AgreementResponder</wsag:ServiceProvider>
    <wsag:ExpirationTime>2009-07-20T23:59:59.000+02:00</wsag:ExpirationTime>
```

```
<wsag:TemplateId>AR_TEMPLATE_v1.0</wsag:TemplateId>
<wsag:TemplateName>Advanced Reservation Template</wsag:TemplateName>
</wsag:Context>

<wsag:Terms>
  <wsag:All>
    <wsag:ServiceDescriptionTerm wsag:Name="AR_TIME_CONSTRAINTS"
        wsag:ServiceName="ARService">
      <ar:AllocationTimeConstraint>
        <ar:StartTime>2009-07-19T19:00:00.000+02:00</ar:StartTime>
        <ar:EndTime>2009-07-20T19:00:00.000+02:00</ar:EndTime>
      </ar:AllocationTimeConstraint>
    </wsag:ServiceDescriptionTerm>
    <wsag:ServiceDescriptionTerm wsag:Name="JOB_DESCRIPTION"
        wsag:ServiceName="ARService">
      <jsdl:JobDefinition xmlns:jsdl="http://schemas.ggf.org/jsdl/2005/11/jsdl">
        <jsdl:JobDescription>
          <jsdl:Application>
            <jsdl:ApplicationName>weather-forecast</jsdl:ApplicationName>
            <jsdl:ApplicationVersion>1.0</jsdl:ApplicationVersion>
          </jsdl:Application>
          <jsdl:Resources>
            <jsdl:IndividualCPUSpeed><jsdl:LowerBoundedRange>2.0E9</...></...>
            <jsdl:IndividualCPUCount><jsdl:Exact>2.0</jsdl:Exact></...>
            <jsdl:TotalResourceCount><jsdl:Exact>16.0</jsdl:Exact></...>
            <jsdl:TotalCPUTime><jsdl:Exact>72000</jsdl:Exact></...>
          </jsdl:Resources>
        </jsdl:JobDescription>
      </jsdl:JobDefinition>
    </wsag:ServiceDescriptionTerm>
    <wsag:ServiceProperties wsag:Name="Service_Properties_1"
        wsag:ServiceName="ARService">
      <wsag:VariableSet>
        <wsag:Variable wsag:Name="REQ_CPU_SPEED" wsag:Metric="xs:integer">
          <wsag:Location>
            declare namespace jsdl='...'; declare namespace wsag='...';
            $this/wsag:AgreementProperties/wsag:Terms/wsag:All/
            wsag:ServiceDescriptionTerm[@wsag:Name = 'JOB_DESCRIPTION']/
            jsdl:JobDefinition/jsdl:JobDescription/jsdl:Resources/
            jsdl:IndividualCPUSpeed/jsdl:LowerBoundedRange
          </wsag:Location>
        </wsag:Variable>
        <wsag:Variable wsag:Name="ACT_CPU_SPEED" wsag:Metric="xs:integer">
          <wsag:Location>
            declare namespace jsdl='...'; declare namespace wsag='...';
            $this/wsag:AgreementProperties/
            wsag:ServiceTermState[@wsag:termName='JOB_DESCRIPTION']/
            jsdl:JobDefinition/jsdl:JobDescription/jsdl:Resources/
            jsdl:IndividualCPUSpeed/jsdl:Exact
```

```
        </wsag:Location>
      </wsag:Variable>
      { further variable definitions: REQ_START_TIME, ACT_START_TIME,
        REQ_END_TIME, ACT_END_TIME, JOB_EXECUTION_STATE }
    </wsag:VariableSet>
  </wsag:ServiceProperties>
  <wsag:GuaranteeTerm wsag:Name="OVERALL_GUARANTEE">
    <wsag:ServiceScope wsag:ServiceName="ARService"/>
    <wsag:QualifyingCondition>
      (JOB_EXECUTION_STATE eq 'Ready') or
      (JOB_EXECUTION_STATE eq 'Complete')
    </wsag:QualifyingCondition>
    <wsag:ServiceLevelObjective>
      <wsag:CustomServiceLevel>
        (REQ_START_TIME le ACT_START_TIME) and
        (empty(ACT_END_TIME) or
          (ACT_END_TIME le REQ_END_TIME)) and
        (REQ_CPU_SPEED le ACT_CPU_SPEED)
      </wsag:CustomServiceLevel>
    </wsag:ServiceLevelObjective>
    <wsag:BusinessValueList>
      <wsag:Penalty>
        <wsag:AssessmentInterval>
          <wsag:TimeInterval>P5M</wsag:TimeInterval>
        </wsag:AssessmentInterval>
        <wsag:ValueUnit>EUR</wsag:ValueUnit>
        <wsag:ValueExpression>5</wsag:ValueExpression>
      </wsag:Penalty>
      <wsag:Reward>
        <wsag:AssessmentInterval>
          <wsag:TimeInterval>P5M</wsag:TimeInterval>
        </wsag:AssessmentInterval>
        <wsag:ValueUnit>EUR</wsag:ValueUnit>
        <wsag:ValueExpression>10</wsag:ValueExpression>
      </wsag:Reward>
    </wsag:BusinessValueList>
  </wsag:GuaranteeTerm>

  </wsag:All>
</wsag:Terms>

<wsag:AgreementState>
  <wsag:State>Observed</wsag:State>
</wsag:AgreementState>

<wsag:ServiceTermState wsag:termName="JOB_DEFINITION">
  <wsag:State>Ready</wsag:State>
  <jsdl:JobDefinition xmlns:jsdl="http://schemas.ggf.org/jsdl/2005/11/jsdl">
    <jsdl:JobDescription>
```

```
<jsdl:Application>
  <jsdl:ApplicationName>weather–forecast</jsdl:ApplicationName>
  <jsdl:ApplicationVersion>1.0</jsdl:ApplicationVersion>
</jsdl:Application>
<jsdl:Resources>
  <jsdl:IndividualCPUSpeed><jsdl:Exact>3.0E9</jsdl:Exact></...>
  <jsdl:IndividualCPUCount><jsdl:Exact>2.0</jsdl:Exact></...>
  <jsdl:TotalResourceCount><jsdl:Exact>16.0</jsdl:Exact></...>
  <jsdl:TotalCPUTime><jsdl:Exact>69932</jsdl:Exact></...>
</jsdl:Resources>
    </jsdl:JobDescription>
  </jsdl:JobDefinition>
</wsag:ServiceTermState>

<wsag:ServiceTermState wsag:termName="AR_TIME_CONSTRAINTS"> ...
</wsag:ServiceTermState>
</wsag:AgreementProperties>
```

Acknowledgments

We would like to thank Michael Parkins for the fruitful discussions about commitments in the negotiation process and the various authors of implementations of WS-Agreement.

This work is supported by the German Federal Ministry of Education and Research (BMBF) under grants No. 01IG09013 and No. 01IG07005 as part of the D-Grid initiative.

References

[1] A. Andrieux, K. Czajkowski, A. Dan, K. Keahey, H. Ludwig, T. Kakata, J. Pruyne, J. Rofrano, S. Tuecke, S., and M. Xu. Web Services Agreement Specification (WS-Agreement). Technical report, Open Grid Forum, 2007.

[2] H. Ludwig, A. Dan, and R. Kearney. Cremona: An Architecture and Library for Creation and Monitoring of WS-Agreements. In ICSOC '04: Proceedings of the 2nd international conference on Service oriented computing, pages 65–74, 2004.

[3] P. Wieder, J. Seidel, O. Wäldrich, W. Ziegler, and R. Yahyapour. Using SLA for Resource Management and Scheduling - A Survey. In Grid Middleware and Services, pages 335–347, 2008.

[4] P. Hasselmeyer, H. Mersch, B. Koller, H.N. Quyen, L. Schubert, and Ph. Wieder. Implementing an SLA Negotiation Framework. In Exploiting the Knowledge Economy - Issues, Applications, Case Studies, 2007.

[5] D. Battré, O. Kao, and Voss. Implementing WS-Agreement in a Globus Toolkit 4.0 Environment. In Grid Middleware and Services, pages 409–418, 2008.

[6] O. Rana, M. Warnier, T.B. Quillinan, F. Brazier, and D. Cojocarasu. Managing Violations in Service Level Agreements. In Grid Middleware and Services, pages 349–358, 2008.

[7] D. Battré, G. Birkenheuer, V. Deora, M. Hovestadt, O. Rana, and O. Wäldrich. Guarantee and Penalty Clauses for Service Level Agreements. In Proceedings of the 8th Cracow Grid Workshop, 2008.

SLA-AWARE RESOURCE MANAGEMENT

Yih Leong Sun, Ron Perrott, Terence J Harmer, Christina Cunningham, Peter Wright
Belfast e-Science Centre, The Queen's University of Belfast,
Belfast BT7 1NN, UK
{yl.sun,r.perrott,t.harmer,c.cunningham,p.wright}@besc.ac.uk

John Kennedy, Andy Edmonds, Victor Bayon, Jacek Maza
Intel Innovation Centre, Intel Ireland Limited (Branch),
Collinstown Industrial Park, Leixlip, Kildare, Ireland
{john.m.kennedy,andrewx.edmonds,victorx.m.molino,jacekx.maza}@intel.com

Gregor Berginc, Primož Hadalin
XLAB d.o.o.,
Pot za Brdom 100, SI-1000 Ljubljana, Slovenia, EU
{gregor.berginc,primoz.hadalin}@xlab.si

Abstract   The management of infrastructure resources in a large-scale environment such as Grid Computing is a challenging task and places significant demands on resource discovery, scheduling and the underlying communication channels. The fulfillment of the business goals and service quality in such an environment requires an infrastructure to cope with changes in demand and infrastructure performance. In this paper, we propose an abstract service-oriented framework for SLA-aware dynamic resource management. The framework provides self-managing, self-configuration and self-healing strategies in order to support autonomic and ambient service management. We study an SLA negotiation process at the infrastructure resource layer, live migration for resource re-provisioning, a multi-layer architecture framework to monitor infrastructure resources and a harmonized interface to access arbitrary sources of infrastructure resources based on SLA requirements. Resource usage will be optimized according to the provider policies and SLA requirements.

Keywords: Service Level Agreement, Resource Management, Resource Monitoring, Service-oriented Infrastructure, SLA Negotiation.

P. Wieder et al. (eds.), *Grids and Service-Oriented Architectures for Service Level Agreements,*
DOI 10.1007/978-1-4419-7320-7_4, © Springer Science+Business Media, LLC 2010

1.   Introduction

The convergence of Service-Oriented Architecture (SOA), Grid computing and Virtualization is creating a critical point for the IT infrastructure resource management. Grid computing allows pooling of computing resources such as computing power and data storage dynamically from different organizations at different geographical location. Virtualization allows for resource optimization by running multiple virtual machines on a single physical under-utilized machine. Infrastructure as a Service (IaaS) is a model that allow a service provider to deliver the raw computing power to the service consumer on demand over the internet through a self-service frontend.

The management of infrastructure resources, either physical or virtual, in such a large-scale environment is a complex and challenging task. The fulfillment of the business Service Level Agreement (SLA) requires the infrastructure to cope with changes in demand and infrastructure performance. IT infrastructure must be capable of adding new resources over time, resilient to failure and provide a recovery mechanism. Infrastructure capabilities such as high availability, adaptability, scalability, interoperability, performance, monitoring and integration are of paramount importance. Commercial infrastructure service provider such as Amazon Elastic Compute Cloud (EC2) [1], GoGrid [2] and Flexiscale [3], provide different proprietary management interfaces to manage their own infrastructure resources. Managing different providers in a harmonious way is a challenging task even though there has been much work on harmonization within the Grid computing area. SLAs offered from the commercial infrastructure service providers are not dynamic, typically non-negotiable, not machine readable and are generally under a standard SLA term. These SLAs tend not to be pro-actively monitored and lack of automated execution of penalties and charge-back.

Our work focuses on the management of infrastructure resources such as computers, networks and storage with an SLA-awareness capability. We aim to solve many of the previously mentioned problems that are exhibited by today's IaaS providers. It will enable an Service-Oriented Infrastructure (SOI) to be mapped to a physical infrastructure and SLAs to be enforced at the resource level. We propose a resource specification that enables the determination of virtual resource requirements in support of SLA negotiation and a harmonized interface to manage heterogeneous compute resources from different computing resource providers. We also propose a virtual machine monitoring component which enables the infrastructure to cope with failure and to meet the SLA requirements. SLA-awareness at the infrastructure service layer enables the identification and triggering of enforcement decisions to protect SLAs, and the ability to carry out dynamic re-provisioning resulting in better service and increased efficiency.

1.1 Paper Organization

The remainder of this paper is organized as follows. In Section 2 we present an overview architecture of the infrastructure management framework. In Section 3 we propose a negotiation mechanism at the infrastructure layer. In Section 4 we present the provisioning and re-provisioning process for the infrastructure resources. In Section 5 we propose a multi-layer resource monitoring mechanism. In Section 6 we study some of the related work. Section 7 concludes with a brief summary and details of future work.

2. Architecture Overview

In this section, we describe the Infrastructure Management architecture of the SLA@SOI framework [4] and the relevant components. Given the distinct responsibilities of the various components within the architecture and to achieve scalability and flexibility, a generic agent-based architecture in combination with asynchronous communication mechanisms (messaging bus) is implemented. To allow communications to route to individual agents, and to distinguish between arbitrary message types, it was observed that assigning one message-bus channel per message type was appropriate. An overview of the architecture component diagram is illustrated in Figure 1.

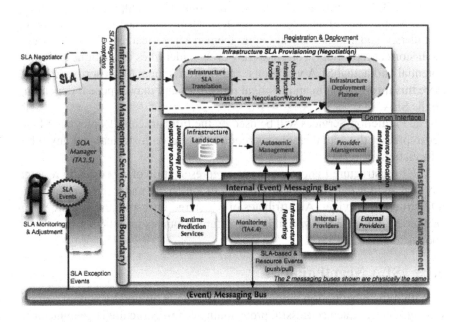

Figure 1. An Overview of Architecture Components

The Infrastructure Management Service provides a customer facing external interface for registration, provisioning, redeployment and management functionalities.

The Abstract Infrastructure Framework Model is used for describing required infrastructure resources and can accommodate infrastructure constraints defined in higher-level business SLAs.

The Infrastructure SLA Translation converts a provisioning request into an Abstract Infrastructure Framework Representation. This could potentially support requests in multiple formats.

The Infrastructure Deployment Planner analyses requests and converts them into individual virtual resource requirements and corresponding software images. It checks if these resources can be provisioned and reserves these resources for a short duration.

The Infrastructure Negotiation Workflow uses the Infrastructure SLA Translation and Infrastructure Deployment Planner to see if resources can be provisioned. The customer may or may not decide to proceed with the provisioning.

The Provider Management component provides a plug-in management system for communicating and controlling resource providers using a consistent abstracted interface. It performs the provisioning and re-provisioning as required.

The Autonomic Management (Optimisation) component sends a request to the Deployment Planner to perform redeployment preemptively based on potential SLA violations identified by the Monitoring component.

The Monitoring component receives events from internal or external resource providers, standardizes them and stores them in a historical repository. It reviews the historical repository, correlates raw events, identifies escalations including potential and actual SLA violations, and forwards them to subscribers. It will store this information in an historical repository and may expose it depending on the SLA.

The Prediction Services will be used by the Infrastructure Deployment Planner to predict the actual resources required based on historical and any other information available.

The Infrastructure Landscape forms a representation of all currently running physical and virtual infrastructure resources which are under the control of the Infrastructure Provider. All attributes of registered infrastructure resources can be queried. Physical and virtual infrastructure resources must be registered here upon activation.

3.   SLA Negotiation

Within the Negotiation module, infrastructure is offered by way of a provisioning service. Each successful provisioning of infrastructure is guaranteed by the SLA specified by the customer. We introduce a template based on the WS-Agreement specification for reserving resources (i.e. establishing agreements), which is customized to size the infrastructure provisioning request according to application requirements.

This template defines the necessary constructs without setting any constraints on the requested values of SLA for the infrastructure. The template includes default values which would typically be modified as part of an agreement offer. It is up to the infrastructure planner to decide whether the values submitted as part of an agreement offer (that was produced based on this template) are acceptable or not.

The Negotiation module would extract the necessary SLA terms and submit them as an argument to the provisioning request. If the request is accepted, an SLA would be established. A provisioning request that has been submitted and agreed upon is deemed to be an infrastructure SLA (iSLA). Our notion of what an iSLA consists of is a vector of three core attributes; a set of terms, a set of Service Level Objectives (SLOs) and a set of rules. The set of terms dictate the resource specifications, a virtual machine in this case, and includes the functional and non-functional attributes that will govern the creation of the requested resource. The set of SLOs are the metrics that are to be monitored by the Monitoring component. These SLOs can be directly or indirectly related to the set of terms. Finally the set of rules are conditional actions to be taken upon the state change of one or more of the SLOs. An iSLA can be submitted in isolation and equates to one resource provisioning request. iSLAs can be combined in order to form a request that equates to multiple resource provisionings per agreement.

In a multi-round negotiation, where counter-offers may exist, the infrastructure needs to provide reasonable alternatives to provisioning requests that cannot be satisfied. This may take place by adjusting some of the terms in the request, by adding extra terms, or by removing some of the existing ones. As an example, one may consider the case of a provisioning request of 2 VMs with CPU speed set to 10 GHz (the Negotiation module does not filter the requests based on their semantics, but rather only on the constraints of the templates used). This request would of course fail due to unrealistic CPU speed requirements, and it would be up to the infrastructure to facilitate negotiation by replying with a counter-offer (e.g. 2 VMs with CPUSpeed = 1.5 GHz), instead of just rejecting the request.

4.   Resource provisioning and re-provisioning

Infrastructure Management needs to be able to interact with arbitrary sources of infrastructure resources. These may be locally installed physical machines, which may or may not support some form of virtualization. Alternatively, the infrastructure may be provided by remote providers such as Amazon EC2.

Following the approach of previous research work [5], we propose a harmonized interface, the Provider Management interface, for heterogeneous virtualized infrastructure services. We develop a technology neutral interface to virtualization technologies which enables an abstract hardware environment to be defined. The harmonized interface enables higher level services to remain separate from details of the underlying technologies that are used in a physical infrastructure, which will orchestrate a potentially unlimited set of infrastructure resources.

The Provider Management interface provides a plug-in management system for communicating with and controlling resource providers using the consistent abstracted interface. Each resource, either local or remote, is manipulated via an appropriate Resource Agent. The Resource Agent is customized for the type of resource being controlled, be it a local hypervisor, or a remote infrastructure provider such as Amazon EC2. The Provider Management interface communicates with the Resource Agents via a messaging bus, which is currently implemented using the Extensible Messaging and Presence Protocol (XMPP) [10].

The Provider Management interface currently provides five basic functionalities, (1) to find suitable physical resources that satisfy the virtual resource SLA requirements of the infrastructure provisioning request, (2) to reserve a virtual resource on a physical resource, (3) to instantiate and start the virtual resource, (4) to stop the virtual resources associated with the infrastructure provisioning request, and (5) to re-adjust or re-provision the virtual resources according to the SLA constraints.

A key benefit of having an Infrastructure Management layer is being able to adjust and reprovision the infrastructure as required. This may be following a request from the customer, or following some internal analysis and detection of an opportunity for consolidation or avoiding an SLA violation.

The type of adjustment and reprovisioning supported depends on the type of infrastructure technologies being used, and the architecture of the application or service being hosted. Typical scenarios include "imaging" a virtual machine and booting it up in an alternative virtual machine, perhaps on different hardware; adjusting aspects of the virtual machine, e.g. the CPU allocation; and live migration, where a virtual machine can be transferred from one physical machine to another, without any downtime for the users. If the application is partitioned according to the Model/View/Controller approach, reprovisioning could simply require the instantiation of additional Views (web servers) or Models (database servers) depending on which component is under the most stress.

4.1 Live Migration

Live migration is a particularly interesting form of re-provisioning as it requires no downtime for the customer. For example, if the Autonomic Management component detects an opportunity for consolidation of services without affecting customer SLAs, live migration could be used to relocate the virtual machines seamlessly if the providers being used support live migration.

However, live migration does not come for free and can temporarily reduce the performance of hosted services during the migration process. The time required to live-migrate can be significant, depending on the size of the virtual machine and network bandwidth.

Some experimentation has been undertaken in order to profile the extra impact that a live migration can have within the running time of virtual machines and the infrastructure. From a host machine running a virtual image, we can issue a command (such as "xm migrate") indicating which virtual machine to migrate, and its destination. Assuming that the user doing the migration has the correct credentials, the machine will be migrated. If the configuration of the systems is correct, live migration will take as long as it takes for the memory of the running virtual machine to be transferred from one system to the other. In our example, a virtual machine with 512MB of memory was migrated in approximately 49 seconds over a 100 Mbps network with almost no noticeable impact on the running services inside the virtual machine.

5. Monitoring

An essential part of an SLA-aware infrastructure is a scalable and self-sufficient monitoring system which is capable of monitoring large distributed systems in real-time. The monitoring system must support two mutually exclusive perspectives arising from the SLA, namely the customer's perspective and the infrastructure/service provider's perspective. The former is interested in the SLA alone, whilst the latter needs to be able to optimize the utilization of their infrastructure.

To help process and manage the volume and variety of monitoring data, a multi-layer monitoring architecture is used. The distributed multi-layer monitoring architecture may be comprised of as many layers as necessary to support the monitoring of the underlying infrastructure. However, these layers have been divided into three logical layers, according to their primary purpose, amount of input and output events, and degree of processing.

The lowest layer of the hierarchy, the data collection layer (L0), is mainly used for the collection of raw input data. Basic filtering and pre-processing of collected information can also be applied at L0 to reduce network traffic. However, processing on L0 should be kept to a minimum to limit the monitoring resource usage.

The second logical layer is the event evaluation layer (L1) that supports the integration of monitors into a cascade of increasingly more complex monitors, ranging from simple metric checks to composed monitors. Composed monitors re-use other monitoring agents to process complex rules, e.g. monitoring of an entire cluster, taking the relationship between nodes in a cluster into account.

The top-most layer, named the service layer (L2), configures and defines the meaning of monitoring events generated in lower layers of the architecture. The architecture prevents top-level monitors from connecting to data collection layer and bypassing the event evaluation layer. The L2 layer is a collection of conceptually similar functions of L1 that provides the services used by any service dealing with the infrastructure and receives inputs from layers below it.

5.1   Monitoring Virtual Machines

There is a need to monitor the provisioned virtual machines. There are several potential sources for the L0 data, but each has its own advantages and disadvantages. In our prototype implementation, we run a generic instrumentation framework like Ganglia [6] inside each virtual machine, and the resource agent on the hypervisor communicates with it via the virtual network. This requires the customer to install, configure and run Ganglia inside their virtual machine, something that will consume some of their resources.

An alternative approach is to monitor the hypervisor hosting the virtual machines, but this only allows the data exposed by the hypervisor to be monitored. Different hypervisors expose different data. Another approach is to install a specific resource monitoring agent, including an instrumentation framework, inside each virtual machine. This would allow maximum control over what is monitored and where it is passed to, but this places some inconveniences to the customer and consumes more resources of their virtual machine than the previous approach.

6.   Related Work

There are a few research projects in the area of resource management in SOA or Grid environment. The NextGRID [7] project introduce a Conversion Factory [9] to map the Service Level Agreements to Operational Level Agreement and a Execution Management System to monitor the execution of the service. SLA@SOI, however, argues for a comprehensive multi-level SLA management framework [12–13] approach that spans across multiple stakeholders and layers of a business/IT stack.

The RESERVOIR [8] project investigates technologies for advanced Cloud Computing and is tasked to provide a software architecture where resources and services can be transparently and dynamically managed, provisioned and relocated virtually without borders. SLA@SOI and RESERVOIR have clearly distinct ambitions. RESERVOIR is focused on advanced infrastructure technologies supporting virtualization and their management across administrative domains. SLAs are incorporated as a specific concern within the overall service lifecycle management at the infrastructure level. It simply seeks to exploit existing infrastructure technologies to bring more flexibility to the service provisioning business. Whilst RESERVOIR follows a horizontal approach on advancing infrastructure technologies, SLA@SOI follows a vertical approach including the complete business/IT stack.

7.   Conclusion and Future Work

As the requirements of SLA@SOI began to emerge, the Infrastructure Management architecture began to be formed and a preliminary proof of concept prototype was developed. At this stage it was realized that the core functionality concerning the SLAs of the infrastructure layer could be addressed independently of the core infrastructure of the provisioning layer. This decoupling allows high-level SLA modeling, management and negotiation concerns to be processed largely independently of the evolution of the low-level infrastructure management components.

Our future plans include supporting storage and networking resources, allowing arbitrary customer groupings, introducing software and service concepts in the infrastructure models, influencing Distributed Management Task Force (DMTF) through suggested enhancements to the Open Virtualization Format (OVF) [14] and etc.

A particularly important future plan will be the separation of SLA management from the resource provisioning system, such that the SLA management system can be used with any sort of provisioning system e.g. RESERVOIR, Amazon EC2. By doing this we will be in a position to provide a system that can SLA-enable most provisioning systems currently in use.

Acknowledgments

We would like to thank the teams at City University and SAP Research for their work on the SLA-focused infrastructure. This work has been supported by the SLA@SOI project and has been partly funded by the European Commission's Seventh Framework Programme (FP7) under grant agreement FP7-216556 addressing Objective 1.2 SSAI "Service and Software Architectures, Infrastructures and Engineering". This paper express the opinions of the authors and not necessarily those of the European Commission. The European Commission is not liable for any use that may be made of the information contained in this paper.

References

[1] Amazon Elastic Compute Cloud. http://www.amazon.com/ec2

[2] GoGrid. http://www.gogrid.com

[3] FlexiScale, http://www.flexiscale.com

[4] The SLA@SOI project. http://www.sla-at-soi.eu/

[5] R. Perrott, T. Harmer and P. Wright. Provider-independent use of the cloud. In Proceedings of Euro-Par 2009, LNCS, 2009.

[6] Ganglia. http://www.ganglia.info

[7] The NEXTGRID Project. http://www.nextgrid.org/

[8] The RESERVOIR project. http://www.reservoir-fp7.eu/

[9] P. Hasselmeyer, B. Koller, L. Schubert, and Ph. Wieder. Towards SLA-supported Resource Management. In Proceedings of HPCC-06, Munich, Germany, LNCS, Vol.4208, pages 743-752, Springer, 2006.

[10] XMPP. http://www.xmpp.org

[11] E. Kalyvianaki, T. Charalambous, and S. Hand. Applying Kalman Filters to Dynamic Resource Provisioning of Virtualized Server Applications. FeBid 2008, Third International Workshop, Annapolis, Maryland, US.

[12] W. Theilmann, G. Zacco, M. Comuzzi, C. Rathfelder, C. Kotsokalis, and U. Winkler. A Framework for Multi-level SLA Management. In Proceedings of Joint ICSOC & ServiceWave 2009 Conference, Stockholm, Sweden, 2009.

[13] W. Theilmann, R. Yahyapour, and J. Butler. Multil-level SLA Management for Service-Oriented Infrastructures. In Proceedings of the ServiceWave 2008 Conference, Madrid, Spain, 2008.

[14] OVF. http://www.dmtf.org/standards/published_documents/DSP0243_1.0.0.pdf.

DISTRIBUTED TRUST MANAGEMENT FOR VALIDATING SLA CHOREOGRAPHIES

Irfan Ul Haq
Department of Knowledge and Business Engineering, University of Vienna, Austria

Rehab Alnemr
Hasso Plattner Institute, Potsdam University, Germany

Adrian Paschke
Institute of Computer Science, Freie University Berlin, Germany

Erich Schikuta
Department of Knowledge and Business Engineering, University of Vienna, Austria

Harold Boley
Institute of Information Technology, National Research Council, Canada

Christoph Meinel
Hasso Plattner Institute, Potsdam University, Germany

Abstract

For business workflow automation in a service-enriched environment such as a grid or a cloud, services scattered across heterogeneous Virtual Organizations (VOs) can be aggregated in a producer-consumer manner, building hierarchical structures of added value. In order to preserve the supply chain, the Service Level Agreements (SLAs) corresponding to the underlying choreography of services should also be incrementally aggregated. This cross-VO hierarchical SLA aggregation requires validation, for which a distributed trust system becomes a prerequisite. Elaborating our previous work on rule-based SLA validation, we propose a hybrid distributed trust model. This new model is based on Public Key Infrastructure (PKI) and reputation-based trust systems. It helps preventing SLA violations by identifying violation-prone services at service selection stage and actively contributes in breach management at the time of penalty enforcement.

P. Wieder et al. (eds.), *Grids and Service-Oriented Architectures for Service Level Agreements*, DOI 10.1007/978-1-4419-7320-7_5, © Springer Science+Business Media, LLC 2010

1.   Introduction

A Service Level Agreement (SLA) is a formally negotiated contract between a service provider and a service consumer to ensure the expected level of a service. In a service enriched environment such as Grid, cooperating workflows may result into a service choreography spun across several Virtual Organizations and involving many business partners. Service Level Agreements are made between services at various points of the service choreography. Not much research has been carried out towards dynamic SLA composition of workflows [2][3][7]. We have demonstrated [9]how a single-layer SLA composition model is insufficient to comply with such a multilayered aggregation of services across many Virtual Organizations and why only a hierarchical structure of SLAs among different supply chain partners can fully describe its behavior. We have introduced the concept of *Hierarchical SLA Choreography* [9] or simply SLA Choreography, in accordance with the underlying Service Choreography as well as the notion of *SLA Views* [9] to protect the privacy of business partners across the supply chain. We have also demonstrated how SLA Views contribute to the process of hierarchical SLA aggregation and how a rule-based top-down validation process can be invoked across SLA choreographies [11].

In this paper we elaborate a hybrid distributed trust system based on PKI and reputation-based trust models to enable our rule-based runtime validation framework [11] for hierarchical SLA aggregations.

This paper discusses:

- the justification and significance of a hybrid trust model for the validation of hierarchical SLA aggregations in section 2,

- the conceptual elements of our hybrid PKI and reputation based trust model in section 3, and

- a use case elaborating the breach management role of PKI and reputation based trust model in connection with the SLA validation framework in section 4.

Section 5 concludes the paper with a summary of the proposed model.

2.   A Framework for Validation of Hierarchical SLA Aggregations

Service choreography is usually distributed across several Virtual Organizations and under various administrative domains. The complete aggregation information of the SLAs below a certain level in the chain is known only by the corresponding service provider and only a filtered part is exposed up towards the

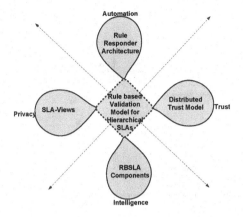

Figure 1. Validation as a Cross-section of Models

immediate consumer. This is the reason why during the validation process, the composed SLAs are required to be decomposed in an incremental manner down towards the supply chain of services and get validated in their corresponding service providers's domain. A validation framework for the composed SLAs, therefore, faces many design constraints and challenges: a trade-off between privacy and trust, distributed query processing, and automation to name the most essential ones. The aforementioned challenges bring in a cross-section of models depicted in figure 1. In our proposed model, the privacy concerns of the partners are ensured by the SLA View model [9], whereas the requirements of trust and security can be addressed through a reputation-based trust system built upon a distributed PKI (Public Key Infrastructure) based security system. Additionally, we use Rule Responder [14] to weave the outer shell of the validation system by providing the required infrastructure for the automation of role description of partners as well as steering and redirection of the distributed validation queries. The knowledge representation techniques of the RBSLA (Rule based Service Level Agreements) project [5] contribute at the core of validation system. Different parts of the WS-Agreement compliant SLAs can be transformed into corresponding sets of logical rules, which are composed together during the process of SLA composition and can be decomposed into separate queries during the process of validation.

A view in an SLA Choreography represents the visibility of a business partner, which in this case consists of a hierarchical collection of its SLAs both as a producer and consumer. Every service provider is limited only to its own view. In figure 2, two different views are highlighted in an example scenario where a client requires to render and host his videos by using online web services. The *rendering and computing service* S_1 is restricted to its view and the client is also shown here to have its own view. The central role during SLA aggregation

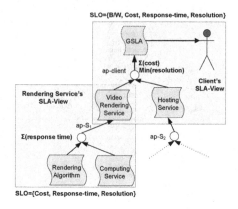

Figure 2.   Example Scenario for SLA Views

is played by small circles shown in the figure, known as aggregation points. An aggregation point represents the control point of service provider. During the aggregation process, terms of the SLAs below aggregation points (called consumer-oriented SLAs) are aggregated within an aggregation point so that a feasible SLA offer can be presented to the client above the aggregation point. The whole SLA Choreography is seen as an integration of several SLA Views. In [9], details of the rigorous formal model elaborating SLA views and various aggregation patterns is elaborated. SLA-views can be implemented by using Rule Responder architecture.

Rule Responder adopts the approach of multi agent systems. There are three kinds of agents, namely: Organisational Agents (*OA*), Personal Agents (*PA*), and External Agents (*EA*). An *EA* is an entity that invokes the system from outside. A virtual organization is typically represented by an *OA*, which is the single (or main) point of entry for communication with the "outer" world i.e. an external agent. A *PA* corresponds to the SLA View of a service provider. Similar to an organizational agent, each individual agent (personal and external) is described by its syntactic resources of personal information about the agent, the semantic descriptions that annotate the information resources with metadata and describe the meaning with precise business vocabularies (ontologies) and a pragmatic behavioral decision layer to react autonomously. The flow of information is from External to Organisational to Personal Agent. In our scenario Rule Responder provides the rule-based enterprise service middleware for highly flexible and adaptive Web-based service supply chains.

Rule Responder utilizes RuleML [12] as *platform-independent rule Interchange* format and has the Mule open-source Enterprise Service Bus (ESB) [13], as Communication Middleware and Agent/Service Broker to seamlessly handle message-based interactions between the responder agents/services and with other applications and services.

As depicted in figure 1, the fourth component in our framework is a distributed trust model. We need to choose a suitable trust model that integrates seamlessly with our aggregation and validation framework. Public Key Infrastructure (PKI) is a popular distributed trust model in Grids. Legitimate members of a Grid are certified by a Certification Authority (CA).

During service choreography, services may form temporary composition with other services, scattered across different VOs. The question of whose parent VO acts as the root CA in this case is solved by including *third party trust manager* like the case for dynamic ad hoc networks. The distributed trust system should work hand-in-hand with the breach management of the SLA validation framework. In case of SLA violation, in addition to enforcing penalty, the affected party is likely to keep a note of the violating service in order to avoid it in future. Moreover, a fair business environment demands even more and the future consumers of the failing service also have a right to know about its past performance. Reputation-based trust systems are widely used to maintain the reputation of different business players and to ensure this kind of knowledge. We propose a hybrid trust model based on PKI and reputation-based trust systems to harvest advantages from both techniques. The main points of the model are:

- the PKI based trust model has a third party trust manager that will act as a root CA and authenticate member VOs. These VOs are themselves CAs as they can further authenticate their containing services.

- Selection of services at the the pre-SLA stage is done by using reputation to prevent SLA violation. Services reputation are updated after each SLA validation process.

- SLA views integrate very closely with the trust model to maintain a balance between trust and security. While the trust model promises trust and security, the SLA views protect privacy.

3.   A PKI and Reputation-based Distributed Trust Model

Trust management can be categorized into: policy-based and reputation-based management systems. The two approaches have been developed within the context of different environments and targeting different requirements. On one hand, policy-based trust relies on "strong security" mechanisms such as signed certificates and trusted certification authorities in order to regulate the access of users to services resulting in a binary decision i.e a party being trusted or not trusted whereas on the other hand, reputation-based trust relies on a rather "soft computational" approach where trust is typically computed from local experiences together with the feedback given by other entities in the network (e.g., users who have used services of that provider). The two trust management approaches address the same problem - establishing trust among interacting parties in distributed and decentralized systems. However, they assume different settings. While the policy based approach has been developed within the context of structured organizational environments the reputation systems have been proposed to address the unstructured user community [6].

The policy-based trust systems are very secure and hence are an essential requirement for the B2B and B2C relationships in virtual organisations and for this reason have been widely adopted in Grid Computing. On the other hand, the reputation-based trust is a lenient approach and are very suitable for self-emergent, automated, ad-hoc and dynamic business relationships across virtual enterprises. In the line of our work, we take the best features of both approaches and propose a PKI coupled Reputation-based Trust Management System. We use Rule Responders' agents to spawn trust across different stake-holders of a cross-enterprise business relationship.

In the following sub-sections, we elaborate how the best features of both PKI (policy-based approach) and reputation-based trust systems, along with Rule Responder architecture, are utilized to our advantage.

3.1   Single Sign-On and Delegation

In the proposed model, a third party acts as a root CA. This third party trust manager acts as a root Certification Authority (CA) and authenticates member VOs. These VOs are themselves CAs as they can further authenticate their containing services. Each member is given a certificate. Certificates contain the name of the certificate holder, the holder's public key, as well as the digital signature of a CA for authentication. The authentication layer in each VO middle-ware may be based on Grid Security Infrastructure (GSI) [8] where all resources need to install the trusted certificates of their CAs. GSI uses X.509 [4] proxy certificates to enable Single sign-on and Delegation. With Single Sign-On, the user does not have to bother to sign in again and again in order to traverse along the chain of trusted partners (VOs and services). This can be achieved by the Cross-CA Hierarchical [4] [8] Trust Model where the top most CA, called the root CA provides certificates to its subordinate CAs and these subordinates can further issue certificates to other CAs (subordinates), services or users.

3.2   Reputation Transfer using Trust Reputation Center

In previous work [1], we have presented a reputation-based model that facilitates reputation transfer. One of the main components of this model is Trust Reputation Centers (TRC). It acts as a trusted third party. The TRC is a

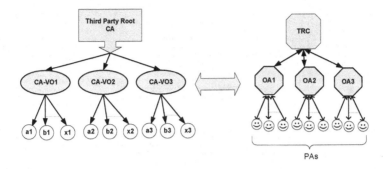

Figure 3. The correspondence between the PKI and reputation based systems and to the Rule Responder architecture

pool of users' reputation gathered from different platforms. Each user, agent, or service can have two values that define its reputation: an overall reputation (trusted or non-trusted for malicious users), and a context-based reputation object (RO). When two users from two different platforms (or organizations) establish an interaction, the TRC can be used as a transparent trusted third party. The hybrid system is currently implemented by extending the Rule Responder architecture as shown in figure 3.

As depicted in figure 3, this reputation-based trust model has direct correspondence with Rule Responder's agents and their mutual communication. The PAs consult OAs and OAs in return consult the TRC which is equivalent to the third party CA in PKI based system. In the rest of the paper, we refer to the channel direction flow between PA to OA to TRC, simply as communication among agent.

The word agent in this context refers to a software representation or a smart service. In [1] we illustrate how Agents can exchange lists of acquaintance agents. An Acquaintance Agent List (AAL) is a list of all previously dealt with trusted agents. Then the questioner agent cross-references the list with its own trusted agents, extracts the common ones and issues an inquiry about the agent in question. The answer is a Reputation Object (RO) that expresses the reputation value given by each agent and the context related to this value. The questioner analyzes the set of ROs and forms a decision whether to carry out the transaction or not. There can be more than one ways to represent trust (e.g. in form of numerical values) and hence there are multiple corresponding interpretation or reference models. So when we recommend someone, the name of the trust model can be used as a reference of what measures our trust, and its degree is based upon. We have also proposed the development of Reputation Reference Trust Models (RRTM) [1] that is used as a parameter when mentioning trust. Reputation is viewed as an object that contains the

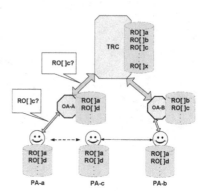

Figure 4.   Query of PA-a about reputation of PA-c to OA-A and then redirected to TRC

context related to each reputation value and reflects the dynamic nature of trust and its change through time. Reputation object contains a multidimensional array, a matrix, which represents the reputation linked with its context and the RRTM used to calculate this value.

```
Object Reputation {
TrustMatrix [context] [reputation value] [RRTM];
Time ValidTime;
Credentials PresentedCredentials;}
```

In figure 4, PA-a that corresponds to *service a* that makes an SLA with an unknown *service c* by checking first its credentials. For this purpose, it consults its corresponding organisational agent, which is OA-A in this case. OA-A too, does not have any information about *service c*'s reputation so it redirects *a*'s query to the trust reputation center *TRC* which then transfers the required reputation object tracing back the same channel.

4.   Proposed Model via Use Case Scenario

Our final goal is to design a framework for the validation of hierarchical SLA aggregations. We achieve this goal by using the hybrid trust system introduced in Section 3. The processes involved in our model are:

- *Validation of complete SLA aggregation*: to do this the validation query is required to traverse through all the SLA views lying across hetero-geneous administrative domains and get validated locally at each SLA view. The multi-agent architecture of Rule Responder provides commu-nication middle-ware to the distributed stake-holders namely the client, the VOs, and various service providers. The validation process empowered by the *single sign-on and delegation* properties of the distributed trust model, helps the distributed query mechanism to operate seamlessly across different administrative domains.

- *Use of reputation in the selection phase*: reputation transfer is required at two stages: at service selection stage and at penalty enforcement stage. In the process of service selection, the reputation transfer helps to select the least violation-prone services, taking into account proactive measures to avoid SLA violations. Out of all the available services, the client (which is also a service in this case) first filters the best services complying its "happiness criteria" [10]. Then the client compares the credentials from reputation objects of the services. The reputation object is traced as discussed in section 3.2. Then the client can select the best service in accordance to its already devised criteria. We assume that out of redundant services which fulfill client's requirements, the service with the highest reputation is selected.

- *Use of PKI and reputation in breach management*: this hybrid Trust is used in the breach management after an occurrence of SLA violation. In figure 5, runtime validation of SLAs ensures that the service guarantees are in complete conformance with the expected levels. Our previous work discusses in detail [11]how the terms of aggregated SLA are represented as logical rules following the RBSLA specifications. These rules are composed together during the process of SLA aggregation [9].

In the scenario depicted in figure 2, the user is interested to render her videos and then host them on the web. Her requirements in terms of Service Level Objectives (SLOs) include a maximum cost of 45 €, maximum response time of 5 seconds, minimum resolution of 640x480 pixels and the minimum bandwidth (from hosting service) of 50 Mbps. In figure 5, we have depicted this scenario from validation point of view. The user-requirements are shown in the figure above the head of EA, as a derivation rule whose premises are SLOs of the aggregated SLA. The SLOs are a expresses as a conjuncted set of negated premises of the derivation rule. The predicates *lt* and *gt* denote lesser-than and greater-than respectively. The agents OA and PA representing the Rule Responder architecture, are shown to automate the distributed query processing. For the sake of simplicity, we outline the Rule Responder architecture just from agent-oriented perspective, and abstract various essential details such as the Rule-bases, the knowledge resources and the role of Enterprise Service Bus (ESB).

During the validation process, this rule is decomposed such that each premise will become a subgoal. This subgoal is sent as a message to the PA corresponding to the next SLA view in the hierarchy where it emerges as a conclusion of one of the rules in the local rule set, thus forming a distributed rule chain.

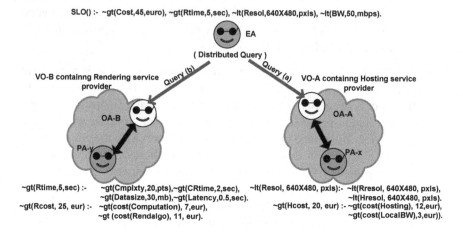

Figure 5.   Validation through distributed query decomposition

The initial steps of decomposition procedure are depicted at the bottom of the figure. In the figure, OAs are shown to receive and track the distributed query whenever it enters a new VO e.g. OA-B receives a subgoal $\sim gt(Rtime, 5, sec)$ representing the requirement that the total response time of the system should not be more than 5 seconds. For each service provider, there is a personal agent. A PA, after finishing its job, reports to the corresponding OA that redirect the distributed query to the service provider's PA that comes next in the hierarchical chain. The single sign-on and delegation helps the backtracking to flow smoothly across trusted partners. The process continues until the query has found all the goals expressed in terms of logical rules or if there is a violation at any step in the chain. Active rules tracking these goals or SLOs, are then invoked locally within the administrative domains of the corresponding SLA views. The true or false results are conveyed back following the same routes. In case of a violation, an active rule is fired for the penalty enforcement. In addition to a fine, the reputation of the service is also decreased by the client service and the updated reputation objects is transferred to its corresponding VO from where it is passed to the TRC. If an alternate service is required by the client then the service can be recommended on the basis of its Reputation Object by the corresponding VO, which also keeps track of other services falling in the same category.

5.   Conclusion and Future Work

In this paper, we presented the design of a hybrid trust management system as part of validation framework of hierarchical SLA aggregations corresponding to cross-VO workflow compositions. The trust system is based on PKI as well as reputation based trust models thus providing a single sign-on and maintaining service credentials based on their SLA compliance. Although the model presented here is strongly related to already existing trust models and frameworks, the application of this model, as part of validation framework of hierarchical SLA aggregations is innovative. We plan to implement this hybrid trust model through iterative development phases as part of a distributed rule-based validation system using RuleML/XML for interchange [9].

References

[1] R. Alnemr and Ch. Meinel. Getting More from Reputation Systems: A Context-Aware Reputation Framework Based on Trust Centers and Agent Lists. Computing in the Global Information Technology, ICCGI'08, pages 137–142, 2008.

[2] M.B. Blake and D.J. Cunnings. Workflow Composition of Service Level Agreements. International Conference on Services Computing, 2007.

[3] G. Frankova. Service Level Agreements Web Services and Security. Springer Verlag, pages 556–562, 2007

[4] A. Lioy, M. Marian, N. Moltchanova, and M. Pala. PKI past, present and future. International Journal of Information Security, Springer Berlin, pages 18–29, 2006.

[5] A. Paschke and M. Bichler. Knowledge Representation Concepts for Automated SLA Management. Int. Journal of Decision Support Systems (DSS), March 2006.

[6] P. Bonatti, D. Olmedilla, C. Duma, and N. Shahmehr. An Integration of Reputation-based and Policy-based Trust Management. Semantic Web and Policy Workshop, 2005.

[7] T. Unger, F. Leyman, S. Mauchart, and T. Scheibler. Aggregation of Service Level Agreement in the context of business processes. Enterprise Distributed Object Computing Conference Munich, Germany, 2008.

[8] S. Zhao, A. Aggarwal, and R.D. Kent. PKI-Based Authentication Mechanisms in Grid Systems. International Conference on Networking, Architecture, and Storage, 2007

[9] I. Ul Haq, A. Huqqani, E. Schikuta. Aggregating hierarchical Service Level Agreements in Business Value Networks Business Process Management Conference (BPM2009), 2009.

[10] K. Kofler, I. Ul Haq, and E. Schikuta. A Parallel Branch and Bound Algorithm for Workflow QoS Optimization In Proceedings of the 38th International Conference on Parallel Processing (ICPP2009), Vienna, 2009.

[11] I. Ul Haq, A. Paschke, E. Schikuta, and H. Boley. Rule-Based Workflow Validation of Hierarchical Service Level Agreements In Proceedings of the 4th International Workshop on Workflow Management (ICWM2009), Geneva, 2009.

[12] H. Boley. The Rule-ML Family of Web Rule Languages. In 4th Int. Workshop on Principles and Practice of Semantic Web Reasoning, Budva, Montenegro, 2006.

[13] Mule. Mule Enterprise Service Bus. http://mule.codehaus.org/display/MULE/Home, 2006.

[14] A. Paschke, H. Boley, A. Kozlenkov, and B. Craig. Rule responder: RuleML-based agents for distributed collaboration on the pragmatic web. In Proceedings of the 2nd international conference on Pragmatic web Tilburg, The Netherlands, 2007.

EVALUATION OF SERVICE LEVEL AGREEMENT APPROACHES FOR PORTFOLIO MANAGEMENT IN THE FINANCIAL INDUSTRY

Tobias Pontz, Manfred Grauer
University of Siegen
Information Systems Institute
Hoelderlinstrasse 3
57076 Siegen, Germany
pontz@fb5.uni-siegen.de
grauer@fb5.uni-siegen.de

Roland Kuebert, Axel Tenschert, Bastian Koller
High Performance Computing Center Stuttgart
Nobelstrasse 19
70569 Stuttgart
kuebert@hlrs.de
tenschert@hlrs.de
koller@hlrs.de

Abstract   The idea of service-oriented Grid computing seems to have the potential for fundamental paradigm change and a new architectural alignment concerning the design of IT infrastructures. There is a wide range of technical approaches from scientific communities which describe basic infrastructures and middlewares for integrating Grid resources in order that by now Grid applications are technically realizable. Hence, Grid computing needs viable business models and enhanced infrastructures to move from academic application right up to commercial application. For a commercial usage of these evolutions service level agreements are needed. The developed approaches are primary of academic interest and mostly have not been put into practice. Based on a business use case of the financial industry, five service level agreement approaches have been evaluated in this paper. Based on the evaluation, a management architecture has been designed and implemented as a prototype.

Keywords: Service-oriented Architecture, Service Level Agreement, Quality of Service, Grid Computing, Financial Engineering, Portfolio Management.

P. Wieder et al. (eds.), *Grids and Service-Oriented Architectures for Service Level Agreements,*
DOI 10.1007/978-1-4419-7320-7_6, © Springer Science+Business Media, LLC 2010

1.   Introduction and Motivation

Being mostly used in academia, scientific Grid computing [1], [2] operates on a best-effort basis for providing and using Grid resources as there are no guarantees of delivered service quality. Moving into the business field, best-effort is no longer sufficient. Even when Grid computing comes to delivering services or making computations to solve complex problems, for which a user may have paid a lot of money, new solutions are needed [3]. Service Level Agreements (SLA) are an essential instrument for commercial service providers to advertise the Quality of Service (QoS) and to manage contracts throughout commercial Grid environments. A SLA is a contract between a provider and a user of a negotiated service. It describes the performance criteria a provider promises to meet while performing a service, states the expectations and obligations that exist between the two parties and specifies the conditions under which a service may be used, for instance, the level of availability, serviceability and performance. Furthermore it sets out the rights and commitments each party has in a particular context or situation, the remedial actions to be taken and any penalties that will take effect if the performance falls below the promised criteria.

The current paper arises from research work which evaluates five SLA approaches in order to establish a SLA-based infrastructure on provider's site. The approaches cover the technical part of QoS and do not match the business service management to improve QoS as presented in [4]. The evaluation leads to a prototypical design and implementation of a SLA Management architecture based on WS-Agreement [5] using the de facto standard Globus Toolkit [6].

At first, we present a business use case of the financial industry in chapter 2 and point out the need for a SLA-based infrastructure. Based on this use case, a criteria catalog is specified in chapter 3 and five SLA approaches are evaluated in chapter 4 for designing a prototypical infrastructure for the given use case in chapter 5. We can just give a rough insight into the SLA Management architecture. Finally, conclusions and future work are discussed in chapter 7.

2.   Portfolio Management as Use Case taken from the Financial Industry

To show the practical orientation of the work in this paper, the developments are based on a business use case taken from the Financial Business Grid project [7], [8]. This use case will act as basis for the exercise of retrieving requirements for SLA Management in the financial Grids domain. We concentrate on the subdomain of Portfolio Management.

Today the financial markets grow quickly and are hard to predict. For that reason investors – private as well as managers in financial institutions – have to be able to analyze quickly and evaluate the risks and performances of their portfolio investments. This might not be overly complex for a traditional private investor who wants to evaluate portfolio performance and only has a small number of portfolios to deal with. Then, calculations of gains or losses can be performed quickly and easily and give relevant information on their investments.

However, in our use case, we face now a financial institution, called "Global Finances", which wants to calculate the performance of around 3 million portfolios. This is quite a challenge in terms of complexity and necessary capacities for electronically calculation. This high number of portfolios makes it nearly impossible to calculate them "in-house" for the financial institution in the time desired to be able to react quickly. Even though Global Finances has a small data center, the average time for these calculations would be in the order of magnitude of multiple days when performed on their own resources. Most of the information would already be outdated once the computations have finished.

For that purpose, the person responsible for portfolio analysis of Global Finances examines the possibility of using the capabilities of Grid computing. He investigates service providers that have the necessary infrastructure in order to speed up the computational process and to drastically decrease the wall clock time of the overall computation. Global Finances has employed virtualization technologies on its own platform and, therefore, is looking for service providers which can deploy virtual machine images. This gives Global Finances better control over the execution environment and facilitates the scaling of the computation. An important aspect for Global Finances is the data management: communication with the service provider should happen in a secure form and all data given to the service provider should be destroyed after the results have been obtained by Global Finances.

The requirements that Global Finances has on both functional and non-functional properties of a provided service can be easily specified in a SLA. Besides these properties, obligations on both parties – for example, the obligation on Global Finances to provide the software to be executed in time or the obligation on the service provider to ensure destruction of left-over data – as well as penalties or rewards can be specified in this way.

3. Requirements on Service Level Agreement Approaches

According to the presented use case a requirement catalog is created. The catalog is based on the special view of the financial industry and the technical view of the Grid middleware Globus Toolkit. The analysis is divided into three main categories which are discussed in the following.

A component which supports **negotiation** between provider and customer is essential for creating SLAs on demand. The negotiation procedure is often based on a template mechanism and defined by a negotiation protocol. The provider manages a repository which contains, for instance, one template for each provided service and prepares a template as an offer on demand. The customer reacts upon this. Parts of the offer can be customizable to adapt special requirements of the customer. In general an offer is defined in a machine-readable language (e.g. XML). However, the customer should edit the offer without knowledge of the meta-language. Similar services should be arranged into service classes (e.g. gold, silver and bronze [8]) which supports a better management of the customers.

The **process of providing** SLAs can be classified into two phases from a technical point of view. First, the contents of SLAs have to be modeled by the specification language and second, they have to be established in the system. SLA systems must support both phases. Modeling a SLA needs a suitable specification language and a service model which contains essential elements defining their semantics. The service model should be independent of a specific environment for describing future scenarios as well. SLAs that are already built and established should be accessible to reuse them or even parts of them as modules to simplify modeling. Modeling a SLA usually takes place in an abstract form which means without binding to specific resources. Furthermore, SLAs have to be executed as automatically as possible.

Controlling the provided service is essential in a commercial Grid environment. Besides an internal controlling, it is additionally done by a trusted third party. Thus, a neutral and objective controlling is possible. The control system must be isolated from the rest of the system and should automatically compare SLAs and gathered information to take adequate measurements. As a result, the whole process of controlling is subdivided into **measuring and monitoring**. Therefore, logical and arithmetical functions must be provided by a query language. Beside monitoring of current values, SLAs have to be parsed and verified on formal correctness. The use of suitable tools eases measurement and monitoring.

4.   Analysis of Five Service Level Agreement Approaches

Various approaches on SLA Management for Grid computing currently can be observed in the literature. As the approaches differ in their complexity and focus on various aspects, this chapter only gives a rough insight of state of the art of existing SLA concepts and tools from international Grid projects. Finally it presents an evaluation of fundamental characteristics based on a criteria catalog in a compact manner.

4.1   Actual State of the Art

Web Service Level Agreement (WSLA) framework [9] is a development of IBM research and promises a SLA-based management via web services. The framework consists of a flexible and extensible language based on XML and a run time architecture comprising various SLA monitoring services, which may be outsourced to third parties to ensure a maximum of objectivity. An implementation of the framework, named as SLA Compliance Monitor, is publicly available as part of the **IBM Web Services Toolkit**.

WS-Agreement [5] is a proposed recommendation of the Open Grid Forum (OGF). It defines a language and a simple protocol for the management of SLAs. For more than the single step negotiation the Grid Resource Allocation Agreement Group (GRAAP) is currently working on **WS-Agreement-Negotiation**, a specification for an interoperable protocol for sophisticated negotiation and re-negotiation of SLAs.

Web Service Offerings Language (WSOL) [10], as a research activity of Carleton University, is an XML notation. WSOL is used for describing multiple service classes for a single web service based on functional and non-functional constraints, simple access rights, pricing data and relationships with other service offerings of the same web service. Describing a web service in WSOL supports dynamic adaptation and management of service compositions using manipulation of service offerings.

Web Services Management Network (WSMN) [11], as a development of HP Labs, targets the management of web services that interact across administrative domains, and therefore typically involves multiple stakeholders. WSMN introduces an architecture, an object model and several components and protocols of a management overlay for federated service management. WSMN relies on a network of communicating service intermediaries, each being a proxy positioned between the service and the outside world.

The last analyzed approach addresses key issues to integrate QoS into web services. The **Web Service Quality of Service (WS-QoS)** [12] framework ensures QoS-awareness during a whole web services communication process. The main contributions of this framework is an XML schema that enables QoS-aware service specifications, a broker based web service selection model that enables an efficient QoS-aware service selection as well as the QoS mapping guarantying the assured QoS.

4.2   Evaluation and Interpretation

This subchapter summarizes the research approaches by illustrating the evaluation. In table 1, a '++' explains a very good realization of the criterion. A '+' indicates a preferred realization and a '−' illustrates that the criterion could be theoretically fit but it is not in practice. If an approach does not meet the given criterion, it is illustrated by a '−−'.

One can determine that there exists a multiplicity of competitive systems at the market. Its development is in differentiated stages or its main points of research are in different sections. Furthermore, none of the examined approaches

Table 1.   Evaluation overview of five SLA approaches.

	WSLA	WS-Agreement	WSOL	WSMN	WS-QoS
Template	+	++	--	--	--
Multilayer Negotiation	--	++	--	--	+
Service Class	-	-	++	--	+
Spec. Language	++	++	++	++	++
Service Model	++	+	-	+	++
Independence	-	+	-	+	+
Reusability	-	+	++	+	-
Binding to Resources	--	-	-	-	+
Automation	++	-	--	+	--
Quantification	++	+	--	+	+
Query Language	++	+	++	+	--
Verification	+	+	+	+	++
Supporting Tools	++	+	+	+	-

fulfills all posed criteria. Nevertheless, WS-Agreement emerges as a quite realizable system in designing and implementing a prototypical architecture. The specification already includes a protocol for the most simple and general case of negotiation: an offer for an SLA is made by either of the two parties and the respective other party may accept or reject the offer.

5.   An Insight into the developed Management System

When thinking about the described use case considering the actual state of the art, we determine that there are lots of possibilities to develop a system for managing SLAs for financial Grid applications. The selection of an appropriate approach depends on the requirements of the involved parties (service customer, service provider, developers). Nevertheless, we can propose a general architecture, mainly influenced by WS-Agreement [5], which enables developers to create a SLA Management System which provides service customers and service providers with a system for negotiation, management and monitoring of SLAs. As a matter of course the proposed architecture is a basis which should be extended and specified to the individual needs of the involved parties. Furthermore, the described SLA Management System presented in figure 1 is usable for the financial industry but it is not restricted to this scope. Especially, when thinking of managing QoS aspects with such a system the range of application is much more broader because of its reuseability for other sectors.

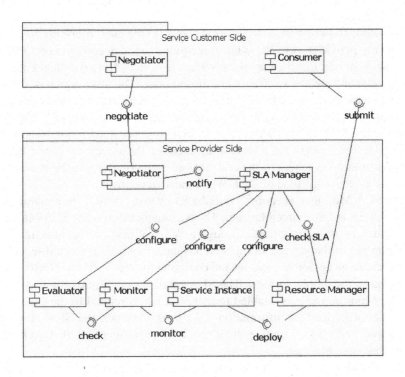

Figure 1.   Architecture of the SLA Management System for Portfolio Management

In the following we describe the proposed architecture for developing a SLA Management System. First of all the architecture contains two parties, the service customer side and the service provider side. A new service can be instantiated by the service customer which may ask for an adequate offer. Negotiator, Service, and SLA Manager are coupled closely together in order to optimize the interaction and perform the service in the best way. The Negotiator notifies the SLA Manager which interacts with the Service Instance as well. The SLA Manager is able to stop the service and it configures most other components. The architecture offers a service and therefore it is possible to construct this as a web service in a Grid environment. Thus, the service based on a Grid architecture offers the possibility to split up components on several resources. A Grid architecture is highly flexible and contributes to the field of distributed computing. The single components of the architecture are described in detail in the following.

The negotiation of a SLA is performed between the **customer-side Negotiator** and the **provider-side Negotiator** according to the negotiation protocol of [5]. The Negotiator of the customer obtains templates from the Negotiator of the provider and creates an offer out of the template. The offer, which is already binding on the customer, can be either accepted or rejected by the provider-side Negotiator. So there is no multi-layer negotiation. If the provider-side Negotiator decides on not accepting the offer, it informs the customer-side Negotiator of the rejection. Otherwise, a service representing the agreement is created, its endpoint reference is sent to the customer-side Negotiator and the provider's SLA Manager is informed of the newly created agreement.

The **SLA Manager** is connected to the Evaluator, Monitor, Negotiator, Service Instance and Resource Manager. The Negotiator informs the SLA Manager on creation of new agreements through a WS-Notification mechanism. The configuration of the service depends on this agreement. The selected sequence of first create an agreement and second configure the service is an effective way of initiating the whole service. The SLA Manager configures the Evaluator and the Monitor and it is enabled to make decisions related to the execution of the service based on information it receives. Further, the SLA Manager configures the Service Instance and it checks the validity of an SLA on behalf of the Resource Manager.

The **Monitor** supervises the system of the service provider. However, it has to be considered that the Monitor is just collecting the data which are sent to the Evaluator with the aim to analyze them.

The **Evaluator** analyses the data received from the Monitor and sends the evaluated data to the SLA Manager. The Evaluator is part of the internal control system of the service to check if the terms of the agreement are valid or if there are violations.

The SLA Management System is connected to the service layer by the **Service Instance**. It is executed on behalf of the customer and related to the Monitor, SLA Manager and Resource Manager.

The **Resource Manager** connects the SLA Management System to the underlying scheduling and execution components. Requests for instantiation of virtual machines and their execution are directed to the Resource Manager which checks the request against the SLA with help from the SLA Manager. Valid requests are scheduled and executed in accordance with the QoS parameters specified in the SLA.

The **Consumer** is a representative entity on the customer side. It stands for any actor in the customer's domain that is making use of the Service Instance. It submits job requests under a given SLA to the Resource Manager.

6. Conclusion and Future Work

Grid computing has gained lots of popularity in particular in the scientific environment. SLAs may be used to establish agreements on the QoS between a service provider and a service consumer. In this paper we described an architecture for a SLA-supported Grid infrastructure. The practical relevance for the created infrastructure results from a business use case of the financial industry. Several SLA approaches have been analyzed and as a result of the evaluation a SLA Management System based on WS-Agreement has been designed, implemented in a prototype and integrated in a Grid environment.

The working group around WS-Agreement progressed already far in its comprehensive development and waits for feedback from practical conversion attempts. Work is needed on all levels starting with the development of extensions such as monitoring the resources involved [13] right through independent implementations to prove interoperability [14] up to high level negotiation of agreements [15]. Integrating service level in WS-RF respectively in Globus Toolkit starts out.

Acknowledgments

This research is a part of the Financial Business Grid (FinGrid) project [7], coordinated by the E-Finance Lab at the J.W. Goethe University, Frankfurt, Germany. This material is based upon work supported by the German Federal Ministry of Education and Research under Grant No. 01IG07004C. Any opinions, findings, and conclusions or recommendations expressed in this material are those of the authors and do not necessarily reflect the views of the D-Grid Initiative or the Federal Ministry of Education and Research.

References

[1] I. Foster and C. Kesselmann. The Grid: Blueprint for a New Computing Infrastructure. Morgan-Kaufman, San Francisco, 1999.

[2] F. Berman, G. Fox, and T. Hey. Grid Computing - Making the Global Infrastructure a Reality. John Wiley & Sons, 2003.

[3] J. Altmann and S. Routzounis. Economic Modeling of Grid Services. Proceedings of the eChallenges conference, Barcelona, 2006.

[4] R. Addy. Effective IT Service Management – To ITIL and Beyond!. Springer, Berlin, 2007.

[5] A. Andrieux, K. Czajkowski, A. Dan, K. Keahey, H. Ludwig, T. Nakata, J. Pruyne, J. Rofrano, S. Tuecke, and M. Xu. Web Services Agreement Specification (WS-Agreement). OGF GRAAP Working Group, 2006. URL: http://www.ogf.org/documents/GFD.107.pdf.

[6] The Globus Toolkit 4. http://www.globus.org, 2009-07-24.

[7] Financial Business Grid (FinGrid). http://www.fingrid.de, 2009-07-24.

[8] B. Skiera, O. Hinz, R. Beck, and W. König. Grid Computing in der Finanzindustrie. Books on Demand, Norderstedt, 2009.

[9] A. Keller and H. Ludwig. The WSLA Framework: Specifying and Monitoring Service Level Agreements for Web Services. Journal of Network and Systems Management, 11(1):57–81, 2003.

[10] V. Tosic, K. Patel, and B. Pagurek. WSOL – Web Service Offerings Language. CAiSE 2002 – Workshop on Web Services, e-Business and the Semantic Web, Toronto, 2002.

[11] V. Machiraju, A. Sahai, and A. v.Moorsel. Web Service Management Network (WSMN): An Overlay Network for Federated Service Management. 8th IEEE/IFIP International Symposium on Integrated Network Management, Florence, 2003.

[12] M. Tian. QoS integration in Web Services with the WS-QoS framework. PhD Thesis at University of Berlin, 2005.

[13] G. Scorsatto and A.C.M. Alves de Melo. GrAMoS: A Flexible Service for WS-Agreement Monitoring in Grid Environments. 14th International Euro-Par conference on Parallel Processing, Las Palmas, 2008.

[14] D. Battré, O. Kao, and K. Voss. Implementing WS-Agreement in a Globus Toolkit 4.0 Environment. In Grid Middleware and Services – Challenges and Solutions, pages 409–418, 2008.

[15] W. Ziegler, P. Wieder, and D. Battré. Extending WS-Agreement for dynamic negotiation of Service Level Agreements. CoreGRID Technical Report TR-0172, 2008.

EXPRESSING INTERVALS IN AUTOMATED SERVICE NEGOTIATION

Kassidy P. Clark, Martijn Warnier,
Sander van Splunter, Frances M.T. Brazier
Systems Engineering
Faculty of Technology, Policy and Management
Delft University of Technology
The Netherlands

[k.p.clark, m.e.warnier, s.vansplunter, f.m.brazier] @tudelft.nl

Abstract   During automated negotiation of services between autonomous agents, utility functions are used to evaluate the terms of negotiation. These terms often include intervals of values which are prone to misinterpretation. It is often unclear if an interval embodies a continuum of real numbers or a subset of natural numbers. Furthermore, it is often unclear if an agent is expected to choose only one value, multiple values, a sub-interval or even multiple sub-intervals. Additional semantics are needed to clarify these issues. Normally, these semantics are stored in a domain ontology. However, ontologies are typically domain specific and static in nature. For dynamic environments, in which autonomous agents negotiate resources whose attributes and relationships change rapidly, semantics should be made explicit in the service negotiation. This paper identifies issues that are prone to misinterpretation and proposes a notation for expressing intervals. This notation is illustrated using an example in WS-Agreement.

Keywords: Interval, Semantics, Negotiation, Automation, WS-Agreement, Agents

P. Wieder et al. (eds.), *Grids and Service-Oriented Architectures for Service Level Agreements,*
DOI 10.1007/978-1-4419-7320-7_7, © Springer Science+Business Media, LLC 2010

1.   Introduction

In the field of automated negotiation, the negotiation process is typically an exchange of offers between autonomous agents [1]. These agents have control over their own behavior and decision-making process. Furthermore, they can adapt to a changing environment, using different strategies and assuming different roles to achieve their goals. When an agent receives an offer, the agent evaluates the utility of the offer to determine the best course of action, such as accepting or proposing a counter-offer.

Offers specify values for the terms that can be negotiated. These terms can include discrete values, such as *{red, green, blue}* or intervals of values, such as *{between 10 and 100}*. During automated negotiation between autonomous agents, utility functions are most often used to evaluate the terms of negotiation. Evaluating the utility of a discrete value is well understood [2]; however, evaluating the utility of an interval of values is an area of ongoing research [3]. Figure 1 shows three possible utility functions with which autonomous agents can evaluate intervals. Using the example of negotiation in the energy market, each utility function can be used by agents in different roles: (a) an interval can have a rising utility, for instance, for a consumer it will hold that the lower the price, the better; or (b) utility only increases to a point and then decreases, for example, an energy consumer can store, for a low price, a certain amount of over capacity in a local battery. At the point that the battery is full the consumer can no longer profit from this cheap energy source and the utility will drop again; or (c) from the perspective of an energy provider, utility remains equal for all values, except one, such as when a value nears a sensitive threshold that requires extra effort to prepare additional resources. For instance, when a second power plant must be activated for only a small fraction of its capacity. Note that roles can change dynamically in this environment. The consumer from (b) can become a producer, by selling the energy stored in its local battery, in which case the *same* interval has a different utility.

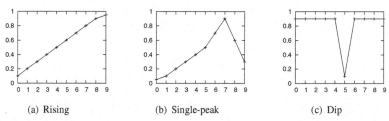

| (a) Rising | (b) Single-peak | (c) Dip |

Figure 1.   Examples of utility functions for interval evaluation, adapted from [3]

Many other utility functions are possible; however, to correctly compute the utility of an interval, it is first necessary to understand what is meant by that interval. It may be unclear: (1) if the choices are exclusive or inclusive; (2) if the values are real or natural; (3) if one value can be chosen or multiple, or

(4) if a sub-interval be can chosen or multiple sub-intervals. Without explicit semantics, the utility cannot be correctly interpreted.

One solution is to clearly define intervals offline, before agents enter into the negotiation arena. Another solution is to create very clear definitions and store these explicitly in a domain ontology that is available to agents during negotiation [4–5]. Domain ontologies are useful in static environments in which the domain of negotiable objects and relationships does not change quickly. However, to achieve automated negotiation in dynamic environments with autonomous agents in which resources are subject to constant change, a different approach is needed.

Moreover, in autonomous systems, agents are able to adapt to changing situations by assuming different roles at different phases of negotiation. For instance, in a dynamic energy market with decentralized co-generation of power, a consumer of electricity can also be a provider [8]. In these cases, no clear distinction can be made between the roles of client and server. As such, the range of possible actions and intentions is more difficult to define in a static ontology.

This notion of adding additional semantics to intervals has already been discussed for scheduling compute jobs on the Grid [6]. Time is an object that is inherently continuous and thus scheduling compute tasks typically consists of defining and selecting not one instant in time, but rather intervals of time. This specific scenario has been addressed by adding semantics to describe two intervals: (1) the duration of the task and (2) the larger scheduling interval between the earliest possible time to start the job and the latest possible time the job must be completed [7]. Whilst in this scenario the specific case of scheduling is addressed, a more generic set of semantics is needed for more general scenarios.

The contributions of this paper are a generic notation to express semantics to facilitate interval evaluation during automated negotiation between autonomous agents in a dynamic environment. This paper is organized in the following way. In Section 2, a negotiation scenario is presented to motivate the necessity of interval semantics. Section 3 presents the precise issues that must be addressed and describes the proposed generic notation for clarifying them. This generic notation is expressed in Section 4 using the WS Agreement specification. Finally, the conclusions and areas of future work are discussed in Section 7.

2.   Interval Semantics

The following scenario illustrates the need for interval semantics. In this scenario, two autonomous agents negotiate the provision of electricity in a dynamic, open energy market [8]. Agent (A) wishes to purchase electricity from agent (B). Agent (B) specifies the available electricity as an offer. This document shows the available sources and attributes of electricity as illustrated in Figure 2. The assumptions made in this example include that *Provider* is an exclusive choice, as a contract is either signed with one provider or the other, but not both. Another assumption is that the *Source* is not exclusive, as a contract can contain both solar energy during the day and coal energy during the night. More chances of misinterpretation become apparent with the intervals *Base Rate* and *Quantity*. The assumption is that the price is continuous with a precision of several digits past the decimal point. However, should a single value be chosen? Or perhaps choosing a sub-interval would be better, such as between 10 and 20. In contrast, the quantity of kilowatt hours is not typically specified with such a level of precision and this interval may actually only contain discrete choices in increments of 1000. These semantics, however, are not explicit and could cause incorrect assumptions.

```
                              OFFER

       Base Rate = {0 - 100}
       Quantity = {0 - 10000}
       Provider = {A, B, C}
       Sources = {Nuclear, Coal, Gas, Wind, Solar}
       Green Percent = {0 - 100}
       Availability = {75 - 100}
       CO2 Compensation = {green investment}
       Buy-back Rate Factor = {50 - 500}
```

Figure 2.   Resource offering

Some intervals may be described with exclusive choices. For instance, *Base Rate* is described as starting at zero, yet this is not a valid choice, but rather an exclusive lower limit. The first valid choice may actually be 1 or 0.5 or some other positive number.

When multiple choices are presented, the order of the choices may have meaning. For instance, *Source* may be ordered according to price or carbon emission. In contrast, when there is no order, it can be useful to express this fact explicitly, as well.

It is also unclear when only one value should be chosen, such as *Provider* or when multiple values should be chosen, such as *Sources*. Regarding continuous intervals, it is unclear when a value should be chosen, such as *Green Percent*, or when a sub-interval should be chosen, such as *Base Rate*. Thus, there is a chance of misinterpretation in both the meaning of the terms (e.g. inclusive or exclusive) as well as the types of choices can be made (e.g. single value, multiple values or sub-interval). Misinterpreting the meanings of these choices can lead to a suboptimal or unacceptable offer.

Often relationships and dependencies between choices need to be specified. For instance, some options may be inclusive, such as *Solar* energy can only be chosen in combination with a second energy source. Similarly, relationships between terms are important. For instance, if *Nuclear* energy is chosen, then only providers *A* and *B* are available. For intervals, the higher the *Availability*, the higher the *Price*. While these relationships could conceivably be derived from several rounds of negotiation, showing them explicitly could make for faster negotiation.

In some cases, an agent may reveal their utility function and/or preferences to its counterpart from the start [9]. For instance, one agent may inform its counterpart that, of the five sources, *Solar* is their first choice, and *Gas* is their second choice.

The semantics of an offer can also change during different phases of negotiation due to a dynamic market: products change and preferences change. A shift in demand could cause green sources of energy to become scarce, thus affecting price. Similarly, providers could add incentives, such as *CO2 Compensation*, to interest consumers in using more gray energy. A domain ontology could not store such dynamic, situation-specific information. However, these changes could be directly reflected in the semantics of the current service offer.

When negotiations are automated, any issues that require assumptions can lead to misinterpretation and an incorrect evaluation of the utility of the offer. As the example above illustrates, these semantics are not always clear. Therefore, explicit semantics are needed to describe the offer being made and the choices that can be taken. Furthermore, these semantics must be expressed in the offer rather than in a domain ontology, so an offer can react to the changes of a dynamic environment.

3. Expressing intervals

Each issue that is prone to misinterpretation, as summarized in Table 1, requires a clear notation that conveys the intended meaning. This notation can be added to service offers and subsequent responses to indicate the exact meaning of a term to facilitate correct interpretation and evaluation.

Figure 3 shows the same offer as before, but with added semantics. To differentiate an ordered list from an unordered list, an ordered list is surrounded by '<' and '>', whereas an unordered list is surrounded by '{' and '}'. To indicate whether an interval's limits are inclusive or exclusive, standard mathematical notation is used. This requires a '(' or ')' for inclusive and a '[' or ']' for exclusive. Indifference is indicated with '∗∗∗'. All other issues use annotations that take predefined values.

Whether an interval is continuous or discrete is indicated with the annotation 'CD' that takes a letter and number as its value. If continuous, the letter 'C' is followed by a number indicating the precision. If discrete, the letter 'D' is followed by a number indicating the size of the increments.

Table 1.   Issues prone to misinterpretation

Ordered or Unordered	Are multiple values ordered or unordered? If ordered, what is the meaning of the order?
Inclusive or Exclusive	Are the limiting values of an interval inclusive or exclusive?
Continuous or Discrete	Is an interval continuous or discrete? If continuous, to what precision? If discrete, what are the increments?
Value or Interval	Should choices be in the form of a single value or a sub-interval? How many of each?
Preference	Is there a preference for one choice above another?
Indifference	Is a user indifferent to the value of a certain term?
Relationships of choices	Are there relationships between multiple choices?
Relationships of terms	Are there relationships between different terms?

Whether a value or interval should be chosen is indicated with the annotation 'VI' that takes a letter and number as its value. If a value, the letter 'V' is followed by the number of values that may be chosen. If an interval, the letter 'I' is followed by the number of sub-intervals that may be chosen.

If one choice is preferred over another, the 'PC' annotation is used. This indicates that the order of the values conveys the preference.

To indicate that a relationship exists between two choices, the 'RC' annotation is used. This takes the value of 'TERM:RELATIONSHIP:TERM' where 'RELATIONSHIP' is a predefined term, such as 'INCREASES' or 'REQUIRES'. Similarly, the 'RT' annotation is used to indicate relationships between two terms. This takes the value of 'RELATIONSHIP:TERM' and uses a set of predefined relationships, such as 'AND' or 'ONLY'.

Figure 3 is interpreted in the following way: *Base Rate* is an interval that excludes the lower limit and includes the upper limit. Furthermore, it is continuous to five digits past the decimal point and one sub-interval can be chosen. *Quantity* is also an interval that excludes the lower limit and includes the upper limit. Furthermore, it is discrete with increments of 100 and a single value can be chosen. *Provider* is an unordered list and only one value can be chosen. *Sources* is an unordered list and two values can be chosen. Furthermore, either *Wind* or *Solar* can be chosen, but not both. *Green Percent* is an interval of continuous natural numbers with inclusive limits. A single sub-interval can be chosen and as this value increases, *Availability* decreases. *Availability* is an interval with an inclusive lower limit and an exclusive upper limit. Furthermore,

```
                            OFFER

Base Rate = (0 - 100]  | CD:C5, VI:I1
Quantity = (0 - 10000] | CD:D100, VI:V1
Provider = {A, B, C} | VI:V1
Sources = {Nuclear, Coal, Gas, Wind, Solar} | VI:V2, RC:Wi:OR:So
Green Percent = [0 - 100] | CD:C0, VI:I1, RT:DECREASES:Availability
Availability = [75 - 100) | CD:C0, VI=V1, RT:DECREASES:Green Percent
CO2 Compensation = {green investment} | VI:V1, RT:ONLY:A
Buy-back Rate Factor = [0.1 - 4] | CD:C1, VI:I1

                          RESPONSE

        Base Rate = [5.5 - 12]
        Quantity = {5000}
        Provider = {A}
        Sources = <Solar, Gas> | PC:YES
        Green Percent = [***]
        Availability = {99}
        CO2 Compensation = {green investment}
        Buy-back Rate Factor = [1 - 2]
```

Figure 3.   Resource offer and response with added semantics

it is continuous with zero digits of precision and a single value can be chosen. *CO2 Compensation* is only available from provider "A". Finally, *Buy-back Factor* is an interval with inclusive upper and lower limits. Furthermore, it is continuous with one digit of precision and a single sub-interval can be chosen.

The response made to the offer also uses added semantics. *Base Rate* contains an interval with inclusive limits. *Sources* is an ordered list ordered by preference. Furthermore, the agent is indifferent to the value of *Green Percent*.

4.   Expressing intervals in WS Agreement

The WS Agreement specification defines a language with which to express agreements and a protocol to support negotiation of Service Level Agreements (SLAs) between parties [10]. WS Agreement uses XML to specify *Templates* that advertise available services and list additional constraints. Based on these templates, *Agreement Offers* are proposed until the parties reach an agreement.

Continuing the earlier example of energy provision, annotations will take the form of XML tags and can be added to the XML schema to resolve issues prone to misinterpretation. Figure 4 shows the same service offer and response using XML for WS Agreement. Two parties negotiate the provision of energy. The provider advertises the available choices in a template using additional semantic tags, as introduced above.

Instead of the '(' and ')'symbols, the *min-* and *maxExclusive* tag is used, and instead of the '[' and ']'symbols, the *min-* and *maxInclusive* tag is used. This can be seen in the *baseRate* and *quantity* items. To express ordering, an additional *ordering* tag is used, instead of '{' and '<' as used earlier. Additionally, a "rank"

<table>
<tr><td align="center">TEMPLATE</td><td align="center">OFFER</td></tr>
</table>

```
<wsag:Item wsag:name="baseRate" CD="C5" VI="I1">      <wsag:Item wsag:name="baseRate">
  <minExclusive="0"/>                                   <minInclusive="5.5"/>
  <maxInclusive="100"/>                                 <maxInclusive="12"/>
</wsag:Item>                                           </wsag:Item>
<wsag:Item wsag:name="quantity" CD="D100" VI="V1">    <wsag:Item wsag:name="quantity">
  <minExclusive="0"/>                                   <enum value="5000"/>
  <maxInclusive="10000"/>                             </wsag:Item>
</wsag:Item>                                           <wsag:Item wsag:name="provider">
<wsag:Item wsag:name="provider" VI="V1">                <enum="A"/>
  <list ordering="NONE">                              </wsag:Item>
    <enum value="A"/>                                 <wsag:Item name="sources" PC="YES">
    <enum value="B"/>                                   <list ordering="PREFERENCE">
    <enum value="C"/>                                     <enum value="Solar" rank="0"/>
  </list>                                                 <enum value="Gas" rank="1"/>
</wsag:Item>                                             </list>
<wsag:Item wsag:name="sources" VI="V2">               </wsag:Item>
  <list ordering="NONE">                              <wsag:Item name="greenPercent">
    <enum value="Nuclear"/>                             <enum value="***"/>
    <enum value="Coal"/>                              </wsag:Item>
    <enum value="Gas"/>                               <wsag:Item name="availability">
    <enum value="Wind"/>                                <enum="99"/>
    <enum value="Solar"/>                             </wsag:Item>
  </list>                                              <wsag:Item wsag:name="co2comp">
  <RC="Wi:OR:So">                                       <enum="green investment"/>
</wsag:Item>                                           </wsag:Item>
<wsag:Item wsag:name="greenPercent" CD="C0" VI="I1">  <wsag:Item wsag:name="buyBackFac">
  <minInclusive="0"/>                                   <minInclusive="1"/>
  <maxInclusive="100"/>                                 <maxInclusive="2"/>
  <RT="DECREASES:availability"/>                      </wsag:Item>
</wsag:Item>
<wsag:Item wsag:name="availability" CD="C0" VI="V1">
  <minInclusive="75"/>
  <maxExclusive="100"/>
  <RT="DECREASES:greenPercent"/>
</wsag:Item>
<wsag:Item wsag:name="co2Comp" VI="V1">
  <enum value="green investment"/>
  <RT="ONLY:A"/>
</wsag:Item>
<wsag:Item wsag:name="buyBackFac" CD="C1" VI="I1">
  <minInclusive="0.1"/>
  <maxInclusive="4"/>
</wsag:Item>
```

Figure 4.   WS-Agreement template and offer with semantics

value with ascending order is added to each element in the list as XML does not natively support ordering of elements. This is illustrated in the *sources* item of the offer. When an agent wishes to indicate preferential ordering, the value of this tag is modified in the offer.

5.   Conclusion

Understanding the meaning of offers is crucial to negotiation. This is especially true for automated negotiation between autonomous agents in dynamic environments. Offers often contain intervals of choices, which are prone to misinterpretation and thus require additional semantics. This extra knowledge is often stored in a static domain ontology. However, this solution is not well suited to a highly dynamic environment of autonomous agents, in which resources, relationships and user's roles are constantly changing. This paper focuses on the specification of intervals of choices during negotiation. The interval semantics proposed are domain independent and self-contained in negotiation offers. In addition to preventing misinterpretation of intervals, these semantics also express dynamic relationships between intervals.

Future work on this topic will investigate how to better express relationships and preferences that change dynamically. For instance, as a deadline approaches, the need for a successful agreement increases and the need for a particular attribute decreases. Furthermore, research will focus on the challenge of adapting negotiation strategies and utility functions during dynamic negotiations.

Acknowledgments

This work is supported by the NLnet Foundation (`www.nlnet.nl`).

References

[1] N. Jennings, P. Faratin, A. Lomuscio, S. Parsons, M. Wooldridge, and C. Sierra. Automated negotiation: prospects, methods and challenges. Group Decision and Negotiation, 10(2):199–215, 2001.

[2] H. Raiffa. The art and science of negotiation: How to resolve conflicts and get the best out of bargaining, Belknap Press, 2002.

[3] R. C. van het Schip, S. van Splunter, and F. M. T. Brazier. Template evaluation and selection for ws-agreement. Service Level Agreements in Grids Workshop, 2009.

[4] G. Tondello and F. Siqueira. The QoS-MO ontology for semantic QoS modeling. In Proceedings of the 2008 ACM symposium on Applied computing, pages 2336–2340, ACM New York, NY, USA, 2008.

[5] H. Jin and H. Wu. Semantic-enabled specification for Web Services agreement. International Journal of Web Services Practices, 1(1-2):13–20, 2005.

[6] H. Ludwig, T. Nakata, O. Wldrich, P. Wieder, and W. Ziegler. Reliable orchestration of resources using ws-agreement. LNCS, Vol. 4208:753, 2006.

[7] D. Battr, O. Wldrich. Time Constraints Profile, Version 1.0. In Global Grid Forum GRAAP-WG, Draft, October, 2009. http://www.ogf.org.

[8] E. Ogston and F. M. T. Brazier. Apportionment of control in virtual power stations. In Proceedings of the international conference on infrastructure systems and services 2009: Developing 21st Century Infrastructure Networks, 2009.

[9] E. Oliveira, J. Fonesca, and A. Steiger-Carca. Multi-criteria negotiation on multi-agent systems. In Proceedings of the First International Workshop of Central and Eastern Europe on Multi-agent Systems (CEEMAS'99), 1999.

[10] A. Andrieux, K. Czajkowski, A. Dan, K. Keahey, H. Ludwig, J. Pruyne, J. Rofrano, S. Tuecke, and M. Xu. Web Services Agreement Specification (WS-Agreement). In Global Grid Forum GRAAP-WG, Draft, August, 2004.

GREENIT SERVICE LEVEL AGREEMENTS

Gregor von Laszewski
Pervasive Technology Institute
Indiana University
2729 E 10th St.
Bloomington, IN 47408
U.S.A.
laszewski@gmail.com

Lizhe Wang
Pervasive Technology Institute
Indiana University
2729 E 10th St.
Bloomington, IN 47408
U.S.A.
lizhe.wang@gmail.com

Abstract   In this paper we are introducing a framework towards the inclusion of Green IT metrics as part of service level agreements for future Grids and Clouds. As part of this effort we need to revisit Green IT metrics and proxies that we consider optimizing against in order to develop GreenIT as a Services (GaaS) that can be reused as part of a Software as a Service (SaaS) and Infrastructure Infrastructure as a service (IaaS) framework. We report on some of our ongoing efforts and demonstrate how we already achieve impact on the environment with our services.

Keywords: Green Service Level Agreements, Service Level Agreements, Green IT, Green Grids, Green Clouds.

P. Wieder et al. (eds.), *Grids and Service-Oriented Architectures for Service Level Agreements,*
DOI 10.1007/978-1-4419-7320-7_8, © Springer Science+Business Media, LLC 2010

1.   Introduction

With the increased attention that green information technology (Green IT) is playing within our society it is timely to not only to conduct service level agreements for traditional computer performance metrics, but also to relate the effort of conducting agreements while incorporating their environmental impact. Much attention has recently been placed on reducing the environmental and operation cost impact of information technology [3],[4],[5]. This includes activities by the US government to especially target data centers, computers, and electronic equipment [1],[24]. As this world wide trend intensifies [6],[16], [8] Green IT will become even more important.

To provide a small motivational overview let us consider a typical desktop computer consumes 200-300W of power. One typical measurement for environmental impact is the resulting CO_2 emission. For the desktop computer this may result in about 220Kg of CO_2 per year. In contrast a typical data center produces 170 million metric tons of CO_2 worldwide currently per year. The expected emission data centers worldwide annually by 2020 will result in 670 million metric tons of CO_2. The average American car emits about seven tons of CO_2 per year. To put this in perspective, the average American family emits about 24 tons. Thus the data centers produce about the same as 28 million people or more than 95 million cars per year.

Another common measure is to simply use the power consumption and relate it to common values. To give an example, today's state-of-the-art supercomputer with 360 Tflops with conventional processors requires 20 MW to operate, which is approximately equal to the sum of 22,000 US households power consumption. In conjunction servers consume 0.5% of the world's total electricity usage and total energy usage is expected to quadruple by 2020. The total estimated energy bill for data centers in 2010 is $11.5 billion. However, 32% of all servers are running at or below 3 % peak and average utilizations, wasting energy spinning and cooling, and doing virtually no work. Thus, it is obvious that any efforts in reducing power and environmental impacts are significant.

1.1   Impact Factors

We distinguish for our purposes a number of impact factors that are essential for our Green IT efforts in regards to service level agreements. These impact factors are targeting hardware, software, environment, and behavior (see Figure 1).

Hardware.   First, we have to recognize that any hardware used in a data center consumes energy, produces heat and thus has an immediate impact on the environment. While a single computer has only little impact, millions of machines as combined in many data centers have a significant impact.

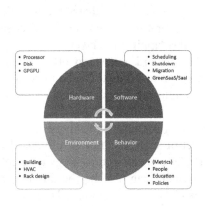

Figure 1. Green IT impact factors

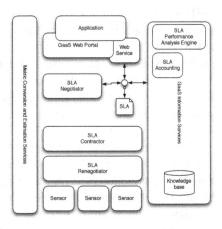

Figure 2. GaaS SLA Framework

Furthermore, we have to consider that the newest generation of hardware includes a variety of sensors and the capability to ingest energy efficient considerations in their uses either through automatic features provided by the hardware itself, or through enhanced software services, which we will discuss later. Presently, obtaining temperatures from processors, motherboards, disk drives as well as modern power supplies and fans and even motherboards have become the norm. Using these capabilities becomes thus most natural to be considered as part of the usage of the equipment. Examples of such integrated features include the shutdown of monitors when not in use (together with software controlled by the operating system), the dynamic voltage scheduling of processors, and the automatic adaptation of cooling equipment.

Furthermore, we also have to consider that recently as part of what has been termed disruptive technologies, general-purpose graphics processing units have been exploited to conduct numerical calculations. The availability of this specialized add on components can provide a quite significant performance boost. For example, we demonstrated in [12]a speedup of seventy times in a biostatistical application for flowcytometry in. This is in contrast to a processor that was available to us as part of our standard hardware infrastructure. Thus, it becomes apparent that is better to use a single system with a general-purpose graphics processing unit instead of building a cluster of seventy compute nodes. Not only do we save energy but also substantial capital costs in hardware. However, one has to develop and find applications that fit such special purpose hardware and it is at this time unclear how to factor the software engineering effort into account. Yet even on a cluster we would have to make sure we obtain or develop proper software that utilizes the hardware in optimal fashion.

Software.   From the previous section, it is clear that the software plays an increasingly important role. We need to distinguish software that we term to be at the "close to metal layer," software on the "operating system layer," software on the "middleware layer", and software on the "application layer."

Each of these software layers can contribute towards the energy efficiency of the underlying hardware. While including sensors and metrics and providing proper optimization mechanisms in order to reduce the environmental impact of the hardware at runtime.

This includes for example the development of sophisticated energy efficient scheduling algorithms [23]. Another aspect of such scheduling frameworks may be the migration of applications or calculations onto more energy efficient hardware. A primitive but effective component can also be the automatic shutdown of hardware or software services if they are not in use. Helping to enhance this trend are Software as a Service (SaaS) and Infrastructure as a Service (IaaS) efforts.

While shifting the traditional programming efforts from developing stand alone programs towards the creation of services, it provides us with the unique opportunity to augment these services not only with capability descriptions in regards to computing such as its functionality or performance, but also integrate Green IT metrics that are relevant for establishing service level agreements between green as a services (GaaS).

We will describe our efforts to develop a GaaS in a later section of this paper.

Environment.   Another important impact factor is the actual environment in which the compute and IT resources are located. This environment includes the building, machine room, offices, heating, ventilating, and air conditioning (HVAC) and reaches as far down as the computer rack and case design. Much effort has been recently spent in this realm including container based compute centers and redesign of backup power systems as for example introduced by Google.

Furthermore, on has to consider where the power for large-scale datacenters is obtained from. Some companies have increased their efforts to obtain power from alternative energy resources. Using the geographical location of the center can also be used to drive down the energy consumption as recently has been proposed by Google moving one datacenter to Brussels. With virtualization, the opportunity exists to engage in service level agreements that take into account such environmental impact factors and schedule Virtual Machines based on agreements which include not only the cost of the electricity, but also how the electricity is produced and which CO_2 value it has.

Behavior.   One of the most important factors that sometimes gets ignored the awareness of the environmental impact one has. Often programs are developed correctly for performance and accuracy reasons, but we have recently shown that we can reduce indirectly the amount of energy used by scheduling calculations on a supercomputer in such a way that lowers the overall temperature. Furthermore, it is not that essential on how fast the calculation is performed but that the overall set of scientific experiments is conducted in a high throughput fashion. Hence the overall round trip time of many experiments is more important than the actual performance of an individual experiment. This concept is well known as High Throughput Computing [14] has been employed by for example the Condor project.

Other behaviors such as using single precision or a mixed precision environment for obtaining results that are good enough could lead to a significant reduction in resources used. Most importantly we observed as part of our educational efforts that the availability of tools to visualize and give fast feedback about the environmental impact of a calculation is a significant feature to change behaviors of the scientists. Reporting on the overall environmental impact of a calculation in terms that can be related to daily activities (such as driving a car from New York to San Francisco) help motivating changes. Exposing this information as part of a computational portal and gateway is an essential component of GreenIT services. Together the activities need therefore included not only in educational processes at an institute level, but also in policy or operational considerations to reduce the carbon footprint. Efforts such as being charged for the environmental impact (for example a carbon emission tax) will accelerate such behavioral changes more quickly.

1.2   Service Level Agreements

As we are reaching more mature frameworks and middleware for Grid and Cloud computing it is becoming more important to incorporate service level agreements (SLA) into these frameworks that act automatically. Several specification, frameworks and software systems have recently been developed that target service level agreements [15],[17].

A good elementary introduction of the topic of SLA can be found in [15]. Important to note are the requirements and phases for an encompassing SLA framework which includes: (a) the SLA template specification, (b) publication & discovery in regards to the quality of service, (c) negotiation between the parties, (d) provider resource optimization to fulfill the contract, (e) monitoring of the agreement, (f) re-negotiation in case the original agreement is violated, (g) evaluation of the agreement to detect violations, and (h) accounting to offer appropriate payment of reimbursement of the services offered. Additionally, one has to also consider that in future one may want to introduce additional monitoring capabilities that allow (i) self regulation and policing as suggested in [21].

A good example of the need for this is a system which makes false advertisements (willingly or unwillingly) for a service that it can not deliver. Engaging in such a contract will be useless and before a contract is established such factors as reputation may have to be put into consideration.

Hence, a SLA framework will have to support these requirements and the associated phases with specialized services that are typically integrated in a service oriented architecture framework. This includes but is not limited to the negotiation of the contract and the monitoring of its fulfillment in run-time, as well as the policing of the contracts.

2.   GreenIT Metrics

As part of our efforts we need to utilize Green IT metrics, such as Data Center Infrastructure Efficiency (DCiE) [18], [11], Power Usage Effectiveness (PUE) [11], Data Center energy Productivity (DCeP) [13], Space Watts and Performance (SWaP) [2], storage, network, and server utilization. Furthermore, we need to expose information about proxies that provide effective indicators and are often easy to implement. Such proxies include productivity sample workload, and bits per Kilowatt hour [13]. We will incorporate these and other metrics into the GaaS framework. This framework can than be used as an incubator to innovative algorithms and strategies while utilizing cyberinfrastructure in an attempt to minimizing the impact of science on the environment.

One of the most important aspects of a SLA for Green IT is to establish proper metrics that can be used for an agreement. There are many metrics available that would be appropriate for consideration. However, we have to recognize that a metric may not be exactly correlated to the final goal of reducing the overall environmental impact. This is especially true if we consider just runtime metrics and not lifetime metrics that include creation, recycling, and disposing of a resource or a system that generates energy to operate a resource. For the purpose of this discussion we do not consider at this time the later.

Furthermore, we notice that the issue of SLAs is actually a multi-scale problem that reaches from the smallest components over a server to an entire datacenter or even an agglomerate of data centers as part of a Grid or cloud.

The most common metrics that we can consider for SLAs are green house gas emission temperature [10] power consumption. Often humidity [7] is also considered as it has a significant impact on HVACs.

Whatever metric we chose, we must be careful if it indeed offers the required environmental benefit. For example let us consider metrics that measure the efficiency of a datacenter, such as the Data Center Infrastructure Efficiency, DCiE or DCE [18], [11], and the Power Usage Effectiveness (PUE): where *PUE = 1/ DCiE = Total Facility Power /IT Equipment Power.*

As seen above, PUE shows the relation between the energy used by IT equipment and energy used by other facilities such as cooling needed for operating the IT equipment. However it does not directly compare the environmental impact between data centers that must be measured in a different way. We find the PUE inadequate for our purposes.

We prefer however to apply the concept of metrics that DCxP introduces [13]: the amount of a unit x consumed to produce a particular work item. Hence, DCeP refers to as *Useful work/Total energy consumed to produce that work.*

To correlate such activities to Grids and Clouds has just been initiated and for example as part of efforts at the Open Grid Forum (OGF) [9].

In general we believe that multiple metrics and proxies that are easier to measure than the actual environmental impact will dominate for the next years the SLAs in regards to Green IT. However, if improved and integrated between each other, we may be able to extrapolate a holistic approach of choreographed services on multiple scales to assess the entire environmental impact of a given calculation, task, or scientific experiment.

3. GreenIT SLA Specifications

The specifications that we need to formulate include typical unit comparison and regular expressions to allow for maximum flexibility. Thus we will allow specifications such as

Establish an execution service for 3 hours if the total carbon emission of the service is below x number of tons.

However we discovered while talking to application users that such a metric, although correct and useful for machine oriented services, may not be enticing the application user to actually use such a service as the unit metric ton may be too unfamiliar or can not be related to a real scenario.

Thus our framework will also include inquiry services that allow to query or even measure a subset of the calculations to be performed the impact of the calculation on a machine. Over time we may obtain a comparative factor for a number of different calculations that can be used for picking a resource with the least amount of environmental impact. This is similar to our efforts that have been conducted more than a decade ago [20][19].

In addition we will have a metric to proxy service that can correlate different environmental measurements that are more easily understood. An example query to this service would be

How many miles can I drive with my car in order to use the same CO_2 value as my supercomputing application that I ran on my super computer.

Clearly such a common formulation of the impact of users not necessarily being experts in environmental units is important to entice the community and to build a stronger relationship to environmental impact of scientific calculations.

4. GreenIT Services

Next, we describe our services for a Green IT enabled service level agreement framework.

Besides providing services that give immediate feedback about environmental conditions as part of a sophisticated sensor network, we also provide services that provide feedback in regards to better utilization and cost reduction of existing infrastructure. These services can be integrated into a framework that over time provides valuable input in how we design the next generation datacenter and encourage behavioral changes how we can balance performance requirements with environmental concerns.

The GreenIT services for SLA are based on a number of integrative activities. This includes (a) analyze and leverage from current efforts in Green IT, (b) project and improve best practices including metrics, (d) provide green monitoring and auditing services, (e) provide services supporting Green IT service level agreements, (f) provide a green portal component, and (g) develop a coordinated infrastructure for Green IT.

Together these coordinated efforts impact how we conduct science with the help of modern cyberinfrastructure such as the TeraGrid and be able to project clues about its environmental impact. As a result we have a positive impact on how modern cyberinfrastructure and datacenters are utilized when clearly confronted with metrics not related to performance or typical QoS methods, but with metrics related to the environment.

Concretely, we design services for each of the metrics we are concerned with. These SLA metric services and than be integrated as part of carefully choreographed web services to utilize the information as part of specialized environmental services to reduce the environmental impact of the infrastructure whale at the same time achieving the tasks to be performed on user requests. Two examples of such services have already been developed. A thermal aware task scheduling service [25]and a dynamic voltage scheduling service [23].

4.1 Thermal aware task scheduling service

We developed thermal aware task scheduling algorithms, by predicating resource temperatures based on online task-temperature profiles [25]. The algorithms can be incorporated into a service providing a better carbon utilization for a set of tasks to be scheduled. Important for this service is that an accurate record of the improvements are kept in order to expose the environmental impact to the requesting consumer service. This should be done not only on a single system basis, but on a Grid wide basis so we can pick an environmentally friendly high throughput scheme to minimize the environmental impact while completing all tasks. We are currently developing some artificial intelligence techniques based temperature prediction methods and data center thermal operation patterns.

4.2   Dynamic voltage frequency scheduling service

Similar to our thermal aware task scheduling service we can leverage an algorithm that we describe in [23]as part of a sophisticated service to to reduce power consumption via the technique of Dynamic Voltage Frequency Scaling (DVFS) of scheduling virtual machines by dynamically scaling the supplied voltages. Some operating system level support for scientific applications are being studied and developed, for example, DVFS enabled MPI applications and multiple module compute intensive applications.

4.3   Integration services

To be successful, we need close integration with other service level agreement component services to provide contract establishment, contract fulfillment, and contract evaluation. The creation of a long-term knowledge base that we can mine through service invocations is an essential part of this integrative activity. Through this service we are able to assess potential service level agreement candidates while at the same time minimizing failures during service execution and service fulfillment. The integrative service will also have the ability to establish a reputation of various services that are offered through it as part of a brokering strategy. Middleware developers are able to register their own services as part of the integration service and their effectiveness will be measured automatically for a multitude of scenarios.

In general our services using this data are under development to serve as a basis for a new generation of more efficient and environmental friendly data centers and supercomputers. The access of the information is managed through control list and group memberships within a federated security framework. Data is exposed through enhanced Web Services following WS-* or the restful service paradigm.

Our architecture to representing our GaaS services and framework is depicted in Figure 2 and demonstrates the integration of the services that are needed to choreograph a successful SLA.

4.4   Portal

A user portal is essential to display the information conveniently and to interactively or programmatically mine it. Users of the GaaS portal will be able to save a *customized and state full view*. We are using state-of-the-art content management portals that are used by companies and millions of users. The Portal components hosted as part of this effort will allow a much more enhanced and dynamic experience while dealing with GreenIT data, in contrast to just a simple portal framework that has become common today. One of the important features will be that the community can contribute custom designed *green* components that can be integrated, even while using frameworks such as Google gadgets. However, we have demonstrated over the last year advanced features that allow us to expose an entire desktop framework through our portal. Hence, we will develop a GeenIT GaaS desktop into a browser rather than just focusing on developing portal tabs and components as shown in [22].

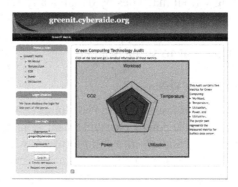

Figure 3.   Cyberaide Green Portal

A screenshot of the integrative monitoring abilities of the portal is depicted in in Figure 3 that shows a snapshot of the environmental control data from the University of Buffalo as well as the calculations associated with it within a simulation that predicts the environmental impact for a calculation to be performed.

5.   Conlusion

In this paper we documented our efforts on integrating GreenIT as part of a SLA framework that considers environmental impact as part of the agreements. We have conducted a number of significant efforts in developing algorithms that can be integrated as part of services decreasing the environmental impact without the knowledge of the users. However, it is important to also develop contracts and services in which explicitly specify metrics unique to environmental impact factors. This allows us to address SLAs not only from an individual server but also from a data center while solving not only a single calculation but a suite of experiments. A history service is integrated into a knowledge base that allows usto learn from past similar scheduled agreements and provide better services in the future.

Acknowledgments

Work conducted by Gregor von Laszewski is supported (in part) by NSF CMMI 0540076 and NSF SDCI NMI 0721656. We like to thank Tom Furlani and the members of the CCI at University of Buffalo to provide us with the temperature data. We like to thank Andrew Younge and Casey Rathbone for their help in finalizing this paper.

References

[1] Report to Congress on Server and Data Center Energy Efficiency. Available from: http://www.energystar.gov/ia/partners/prod_development/downloads/EPA_Da tacenter_Report_Congress_Final1.pdf.

[2] SWaP (Space, Watts and Performance) Metric. Web Page. Available from: http://www.sun.com/servers/coolthreads/swap/.

[3] Green IT definition. Webpage, May 2008. Available from: http://en.wikipedia.org/wiki/Green_computing.

[4] Green IT definition. Webpage, May 2008. Available from: http://thefutureofthings.com/articles/1003/green-computing.html.

[5] Green IT definition. Webpage, May 2008. Available from: http://www.webopedia.com/TERM/G/Green_IT.html.

[6] California government goes green. Website, 2009. Available from: http://www.arb.ca.gov/oss/green/greencites.htm.

[7] Data center humidity levels source of debate. Website, June 2009. Available from: http://searchdatacenter.techtarget.com/news/article/0,289142,sid80_gci1261265,00.html.

[8] EU energy star. Website, 2009. Available from: http://www.eu-energystar.org/en/en_database.htm.

[9] Metrics and an API for Green Computing on the Cloud. Website, May 2009. Available from: http://www.ogf.org/gf/event_schedule/index.php?id=1704.

[10] Recommended Data Center Temperature & Humidity. Website, June 2009. Available from: http://www.avtech.com/About/Articles/AVT/NA/All/-/DD-NN-AN-TN/Recommended_Computer_Room_Temperature_Humidity.htm.

[11] C. Belady. The Green Grid Data center Efficiency Metrics: PUE and DCIE. Technical report, The Green Grid, Feb. 2007.

[12] J. Espenshade, A. Pangborn, J. Cavenaugh, G. von Laszewski, and D. Roberts. Accelerating Partitional Algorithms for Flow Cytometry on GPUs. In The 7th IEEE International Symposium on Parallel and Distributed Processing with Applications (ISPA-09), Chengdu and Jiuzhai Valley, China, IEEE, August 2009.

[13] J. Haas et al. A Framework for Data Center Energy Productivity. Technical report, The Green Grid, Feb. 2008.

[14] S. Fields. Hunting for Wasted Computing Power: New Software for Computing Networks Puts Idle PC's to Work. University of Wisconsin Research Sampler, 1993. Available from: http://www.cs.wisc.edu/condor/doc/WiscIdea.html.

[15] Gridpedia. Service Level Agreements. Available from: http://www.gridipedia.eu/sla-article.html.

[16] J. Kirk. EU to study energy use by data centers. Website, Feb. 2007. Available from: http://www.networkworld.com/news/2007/022307-eu-to-study-energy-use.html.

[17] SOI. Service Level Agreements. Available from: http://sla-at-soi.eu/.

[18] G. Verdun. The Green Grid metrics: Data center infrastructure efficiency (DCiE) detailed anaysis. Technical report, The Green Grid, Feb. 2007.

[19] G. von Laszewski. An Interactive Parallel Programming Environment Applied in Atmo-
      spheric Science. In G.-R. Hoffman and N. Kreitz, editors, *Making Its Mark, Proceedings of
      the 6th Workshop on the Use of Parallel Processors in Meteorology*, pages 311–325, Read-
      ing, UK, European Centre for Medium Weather Forecast, World Scientific. 2-6 December
      1996.

[20] G. von Laszewski. A Loosely Coupled Metacomputer: Cooperating Job Submissions
      Across Multiple Supercomputing Sites. Concurrency, Experience, and Practice, 11(5):933–
      948, December 1999. The initial version of this paper was available in 1996.

[21] G. von Laszewski, B. Alunkal, and I. Veljkovic. Toward Reputable Grids. Scalable
      Computing: Practice and Experience, 6(3):95–106, September 2005.

[22] G. von Laszewski, F. Wang, A. Younge, X. He, Z. Guo, and M. Pierce. Cyberaide
      JavaScript: A JavaScript Commodity Grid Kit. In GCE08 at SC'08, Austin, TX, IEEE,
      Nov. 16 2008. Available from: http://cyberaide.googlecode.com/svn/trunk/papers/08-
      javascript/vonLaszewski-08-javascript.pdf.

[23] G. von Laszewski, L. Wang, A.J. Younge, and X. He.   Power-Aware
      Scheduling of Virtual Machines in DVFS-enabled Clusters.   In IEEE Clus-
      ter 2009, New Orleans, IEEE; 31 Aug. – Sep. 4 2009.   Available from:
      http://code.google.com/p/cyberaide/source/browse/trunk/papers/09-greenit-
      cluster09/vonLaszewski-cluster09.pdf.

[24] D. Wang. Meeting green computing challenges. In International Symposium on High
      Density packaging and Microsystem Integration, pages 1–4, June 2007.

[25] L. Wang, G. von Laszewski, J. Dayal, X. He, A.J. Younge, and T.R. Furlani.
      Towards Thermal Aware Workload Scheduling in a Data Center.   In Proceed-
      ings of the 10th International Symposium on Pervasive Systems, Algorithms and
      Networks (ISPAN2009), Kao-Hsiung, Taiwan, 14-16 December 2009.   Available
      from: http://cyberaide.googlecode.com/svn/trunk/papers/09-greenit-ispan1/vonLaszewski-
      ispan1.pdf.

EXTENDING WS-AGREEMENT WITH MULTI-ROUND NEGOTIATION CAPABILITY

Angela Rumpl, Oliver Wäldrich, Wolfgang Ziegler
Department of Bioinformatics
Fraunhofer Institute SCAI
53754 Sankt Augustin, Germany
{angela.rumpl, oliver.waeldrich, wolfgang.ziegler}@scai.fraunhofer.de

Abstract   The WS-Agreement specification of the Open Grid Forum defines a language and a protocol for advertising the capabilities of service providers and creating agreements based on templates, and for monitoring agreement compliance at runtime. While the specification, which currently is in the process of transition from a proposed recommendation of the Open Grid Forum to a full recommendation, has been widely used after the initial publication in May 2007, it became obvious that the missing possibility to negotiate an agreement rather than just accepting an offer is limiting or inhibiting the use of WS-Agreement for a number of use-cases. Therefore, the Grid Resource Allocation Agreement Working Group of the Open Grid Forum started in 2008 to prepare an extension of WS-Agreement that adds negotiation capabilities without changing the current specification in a way, which leads to an incompatible new version of WS-Agreement. In this paper we present the results of this process with an updated version of the specification in mind and the first implementation in the European project SmartLM.

Keywords: Service Level Agreement, WS-Agreement, Negotiation

P. Wieder et al. (eds.), *Grids and Service-Oriented Architectures for Service Level Agreements,*
DOI 10.1007/978-1-4419-7320-7_9, © Springer Science+Business Media, LLC 2010

1.   Introduction

Service Level Agreements (SLA) are used in different domains and on different levels to establish agreements on the quality of a service (QoS) between a service provider and a service consumer. SLAs can be based on general agreements, e.g. framework agreements (paper contracts), that govern the relationship between parties, may include also legal aspects and may set boundaries for SLAs. In this paper we only consider dynamic agreements, which are created electronically on demand between programs acting on behalf of the service provider and service consumer.

The WS-Agreement specification defines a language and a protocol for advertising the capabilities of service providers and creating agreements based on templates, and for monitoring agreement compliance at runtime, thus, providing an framework for creating SLAs. The specification has been published as a proposed recommendation by the Open Grid Forum (OGF) May 2007 and currently is in transition to becoming a full recommendation. WS-Agreement has been and is widely used since 2006 in an number of European and National projects [6, 11]. However, it turned out that the missing capability of WS-Agreement for multi-round negotiation of the terms of an agreement limits its usability for certain use cases where an agreement can not be reached in a single step as stipulated by the current version of WS-Agreement. For example, if the offer can not be fulfilled exactly by the provider but the provider would benefit from making a counter offer indicating the terms of the service that could be delivered. Or, the customer requires multiple services from different providers to fulfill a single task, in which case the availability of the different services has to be negotiated. Besides approaches to define more generic negotiation frameworks, e.g. in the context of the NextGRID project [10, 3] a number of individuals and projects worked on extensions of WS-Agreement over the last three years to overcome this limitation . Some of them focus on the initial negotiation before an agreement is created [1, 4, 14, 9], while other investigate solutions for re-negotiation to modify service level objectives at a later stage when the agreement is in force already [5, 2]. Early 2008 the Grid Resource Allocation Agreement Working Group (GRAAP-WG) of the Open Grid Forum started to discuss and work on an extension of WS-Agreement that adds negotiation capabilities taking into account the preparatory work mentioned before. The GRAAP-WG decided to stay in compliant to the current specification and not to develop extensions, which lead to an incompatible new version of WS-Agreement. In this paper we present the results of this process with a updated and compliant version of the specification in mind and report from the first implementation in the European project SmartLM.

The remainder of the paper is organized as follows. In Section 2 gives a brief overview on core aspects of the current WS-Agreement Section specification, Section 3 presents use-cases for negotiation. Protocol and messages for negotiation of agreements are introduced in Section 4. Section 5 describes the first implementation of the protocol in the European SmartLM project and Section 6 concludes the paper and gives a brief outlook on future work.

2. WS-Agreement Version 1.0

In this section we present a brief overview of the current version of WS-Agreement, e.g. the structure, the protocol, the state-machine.

The Web Services Agreement Specification Version 1.0 [13] from the Open Grid Forum (OGF) describes a protocol for establishing an agreement on the usage of Services between a service provider and a consumer. It defines a language and a protocol to represent the services of providers, create agreements based on offers and monitor agreement compliance at runtime. An agreement defines a relationship between two parties that is dynamically established and dynamically managed. The objective of this relationship is to deliver a service by one of the parties. In the agreement each party agrees on the respective roles, rights and obligations.

A provider in an agreement offers a service according to conditions described in the agreement. A consumer enters into an agreement with the intent of obtaining guarantees on the availability of one or more services from the provider. Agreements can also be negotiated by entities acting on behalf the provider and / or the consumer. An agreement creation process usually consists of three steps: The initiator (often the service or resource consumer) retrieves a template from the responder (often the service or resource provider), which advertises the types of offers the responder is willing to accept. The initiator then makes an offer, which is either accepted or rejected by the responder.

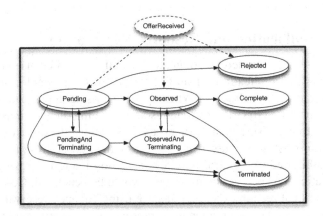

Figure 1. WS-Agreement Version 1.0 state machine

The underlying protocol as specified in WS-Agreement version 1.0 does not contain elements to allow further negotiation based on an initial offer. Especially, the responder has no possibility to reply with a counter offer, which could express more precise the SLOs a provider is able to fulfill at that time. Thus, once the initial offer is rejected by the responder, the only was to continue for the initiator is guessing which part of the offer can not be fulfilled, modifying the offer accordingly and sending the offer to the responder again. Obviously, a tedious process with limited chances to reach an agreement especially if the agreement contains variable terms that have to be agreed upon, e.g. the time when a certain service is required, or if there are multiple QoS objectives to be reached. The agreement states as proposed in the WS-Agreement protocol version 1.0 are depicted in Figure 1.

An agreement consists of the agreement name, its context and the agreement terms. The context contains information about the involved parties and metadata such as the duration of the agreement. Agreement terms define the content of an agreement: Service Description Terms (SDTs) define the functionality that is delivered under an agreement. A SDT includes a domain-specific description of the offered or required functionality (the service itself). Guarantee Terms define assurance on service quality of the service described by the SDTs. They define Service Level Objectives (SLOs), which describe the quality of service aspects of the service that have to be fulfilled by the provider. The Web Services Agreement Specification allows the usage of any domain specific or standard condition expression language to define SLOs. The specification of domain-specific term languages is explicitly left open.

3.   Use-Cases for negotiation

In this section we present three use cases where negotiation is required to create SLAs .

3.1   Co-allocation and Resource Reservation

When running a commercial application usually a valid license is required for executing the application. This license has to be available, during the application start-up for validation. When a job comprising the execution of such a license is submitted to Grid or Cloud resources the middleware must provide mechanisms to make sure, that the license is available at the execution site. In order to avoid wasting resources, e.g. blocking the license from the moment the job is submitted to the Grid middleware, co-ordination of reservation of the computational resources and the license would be beneficial. Co-allocating the computational resources and the license using advance reservation helps achieving this goal. The reservation properties can be considered and expressed as Quality of Service terms and SLAs are created for the reservation SLOs once the service provider is able to fix and guarantee the reservation. In the SmartLM project [12] this is done by the MetaScheduling Service (MSS), which negotiates the time-slot with the scheduler of the resource providers and the SmartLM License Management Service Service. After successful negotiation the resources requested by the user both computational resources and the license are reserved.

3.2 Agreement on multiple QoS Parameters

In an environment consisting of several clusters potentially operated in different administrative domains SLAs might be used for co-allocation or the resource allocation for workflows. A typical use-case is the co-allocation of multiple computing resources with specific properties together with network links with a dedicated QoS between these resources to run a distributed parallel application. The user specifies his request and the resource orchestrator starts negotiating with the local scheduling systems of the computing resources and the network RMS (NRMS) in order to find a suitable time-slot where the availability of all resources with the requested QoS parameters can be guaranteed for the same time period. Once a common time-slot is identified the orchestrator requires the reservation of the individual resources [7]. Again, the reservation properties can be expressed as parameters of the QoS and an SLA is created for the reservation. In the PHOSPHORUS project [8] this is done by the MSS, which negotiates the time-slots and the QoS with the different schedulers of the clusters and the NRMS and initiates the reservation of all resources requested by the user. Another use-case is a workflow spanning across several resources. The only difference to the use-case described before is the type of temporal dependencies: While for the distributed parallel application the resources must be reserved for the same time, for the workflow use-case the resources are needed in a sequence given by the workflow.

3.3 Grid Scheduler interoperation

As there is no single orchestrating service or Grid scheduler in a Grid spanning across countries and administrative domains we have to deal with multiple instances of independent Grid schedulers. Using resources from different domains requires co-ordination across multiple sites. There are two approaches either directly trying to negotiate with respective local scheduling systems or negotiation with the respective local orchestrator. The former solution requires local policies allowing a remote orchestrator to negotiate with local schedulers, which is in general not the case. In the second case there is one access point to the local resources, which then negotiates on behalf of the initiation orchestrator. As the second approach also has a better scalability than the first one this approach is currently implemented in the German D-Grid project DGSI (D-Grid

Scheduling Interoperability). For the communication between the different orchestration services or Grid schedulers in D-Grid WS-Agreement has been selected as language and protocol to create the SLAs.

4.   Protocol and messages for WS-Agreement-Negotiation

The built-in negotiation capabilities of WS-Agreement as specified in version 1.0 are limited to a simple offer accept/reject procedure. Thus, either party can send an offer and the respective other party may accept this offer or reject it. To overcome this limitation, a negotiation process was defined by the GRAAP working group of the Open Grid Forum that allows negotiation on top of WS-Agreement without requiring incompatible changes of WS-Agreement. The resulting protocol extensions are described in the following sections while referring to the specifics of the SmartLM environment where appropriate. Figure 2 presents an overview of the negotiation process.

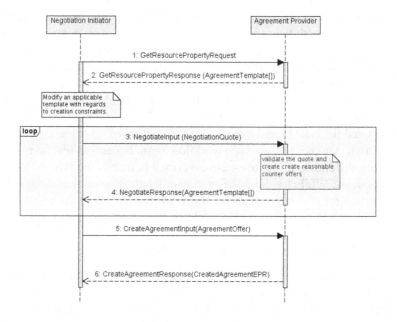

Figure 2.   Overview of the negotiation process.

4.1   Initialisation of the negotiation process

First, the negotiation initiator initializes the process by querying a set of SLA templates from agreement providers sending a standard WS-Agreement message (the getResourceProperty request) to agreement providers. Within the SmartLM environment, any resource scheduler or any client who wants to reserve a license will be the negotiation initiator and any SmartLM server can act as an agreement provider. In general, the agreement provider uses site-specific mechanisms to advertise the available templates and to provide access to them. The terms in the templates are site-specific, e.g. a resource provider for computing resources would provide templates with using JSDL as term language, while templates from a license server contain terms needed to describe to licenses it manages. The initiator, in SmartLM the user, chooses the most suitable template as a starting point for the negotiation process. Thus, here the most suitable template is determined by the user who is expected to select the template containing terms, e.g. properties of a license, which the user intends to use. This template defines the context of the subsequent iterations. All subsequent offers must refer to this agreement template. This is required in order to enable an agreement provider to validate the creation constraints of the original template during the negotiation process, and therefore the validity of an offer.

4.2   Negotiation of the template

After the negotiation initiator has chosen an agreement template, it (the user's client acting as agreement initiator on behalf of the user now) will create a new negotiation quote based on the chosen template. This quote must contain a reference to the originating template within its context. Furthermore, the agreement initiator may adjust the content of the quote, i.e. service description terms, the service property terms, and the guarantee terms. These changes must be done according to the creation constraints defined in the original template.

After the initiator created the negotiation quote according to its requirements, it is send to responders via a negotiate message. Now the agreement provider checks whether the service defined in the request could be provided or not. If the service can be provided, it just returns an agreement template to the client, indicating that an offer based on that template will potentially be accepted. Otherwise, the provider employs some strategy to create reasonable counter offers.

The relationship between dynamically created templates and original ones must be reflected by updating the context of the new templates accordingly. After creating the counter offers the provider sends them back to the negotiation initiator (negotiate response).

WS-Agreement-Negotiation does not provide strategies for support of negotiations, this is beyond the scope of the specification. However, it provides the basic multi-round negotiation mechanisms, which can be used to create sophisticated strategies, like e.g. auctions or such developed in the agents community.

4.3   Post-processing of the templates

After the negotiation initiator received the counter offers (templates) from the negotiation responder, it checks whether one or more meets its requirements. Sending multiple counter offers allow to speed up the negotiation process but it is not mandatory for the negotiation responder to send more than one counter offer. If there is no such template, the initiator can either stop the negotiation process, or start again from step 4.1. If there is an applicable template, the initiator validates whether there is need for an additional negotiation step or not. If yes, the initiator uses the selected template and proceeds with step 4.2, otherwise the selected template is used to create a new SLA.

4.4   Negotiation Messages

New messages were defined as an extension of the WS-Agreement messages to cover the negotiation process.

Listing 1: Negotiate Messages

```
<wsdl:message name="NegotiateInputMessage">
  <wsdl:part element="wsag−neg:NegotiateInput" name="parameters"/>
</wsdl:message>

<wsdl:message name="NegotiateOuputMessage">
  <wsdl:part element="wsag−neg:NegotiateResponse" name="parameters"/>
</wsdl:message>
```

To start the negotiation process, the initiator sends a NegotiateInputMessage. The NegotiateInputMessage expects as Input a NegotiateInputType, which must hold a NegotiationQuote.

The next listing describes the xml schema definition of the necessary types. The NegotiateInputType contains a NegotiationQuote element, which is of type AgreementType. The NegotiateOutputType contains an unbounded amount of Template elements of type AgreementTemplateType.

Listing 2: Schema Types

```
<xs:element name="NegotiateInput" type="wsag−neg:NegotiateInputType"/>
<xs:element name="NegotiateResponse" type="wsag−neg:NegotiateOutputType"/>
<xs:element name="NegotiationQuote" type="wsag:AgreementType"/>
<xs:complexType name="NegotiateInputType">
<xs:sequence>
  <xs:element ref="wsag−neg:NegotiationQuote" maxOccurs="1" minOccurs="1"/>
  <xs:any namespace="##other" processContents="lax" maxOccurs="unbounded"
        minOccurs="0"/>
</xs:sequence>
</xs:complexType>
<xs:complexType name="NegotiateOutputType">
```

```
<xs:sequence>
  <xs:element name="Template" type="wsag:AgreementTemplateType"
      maxOccurs="unbounded" minOccurs="1"/>
  <xs:any namespace="##other" processContents="lax" maxOccurs="unbounded"
      minOccurs="0" />
</xs:sequence>
</xs:complexType>
```

5. Implementation of WS-Agreement-Negotiation in SmartLM

In order to implement WS-Agreement and WS-Agreement-Negotiation, the SmartLM component SLA and Negotiation Service uses the WS-Agreement Framework for Java (WSAG4J) [4]. WSAG4J implements the basic features of the WS-Agreement protocol and also the WS-Negotiation extension described in Section 4. Furthermore, it uses a number of standards in conjunction with WS-Agreement to provide a complete development framework for SLA based services.

5.1 WS-Agreement Framework for Java (WSAG4J)

In WSAG4J agreements are created based on specific templates. Therefore, a client queries the agreement templates from an agreement factory. Based on a suitable template a client creates a new agreement offer, and may modify the offer. The offer is then sent to the agreement factory that will create a new agreement. It is also possible for the client to initialize a negotiation process by sending a negotiation quote before creating an agreement offer.

When the WSAG4J agreement factory receives a create agreement request, it will first lookup the template that was used to create the agreement offer. This template must be specified within the agreement context of the agreement offer. Each template is uniquely identified by its name and its template id. The template id identifies the version of the template and the action used to create the agreement.

The WSAG4J engine allows deploying a set of agreement factory actions per agreement factory. Each factory action comprises a GetTemplateAction, a NegotiateAction, and a CreateAgreementAction. The GetTemplateAction returns exactly one agreement template. Therefore, one specific agreement template is identified by its template name and its template id and maps exactly to one specific agreement factory action.

Based on a specific template, either a negotiation process can be started, or an agreement can be created. E.g. when a client creates a new agreement offer based on an agreement template, the offer contains a reference to the template within the AgreementContext. When a create agreement request was received by a WSAG4J server, the WSAG4J engine will look up the associated agreement factory action, validate the incoming offer against the creation constraints defined in the template that was used to create the offer, and invoke the according CreateAgreementAction.

5.2   SLA and Negotiation Service

The SLA and Negotiation Service implements the WSAG4J engine and exposes an agreement factory that provides to the user when requesting a template exactly one agreement template. This template holds the xml structure of a license agreement including creation constraints.

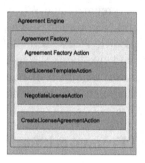

Figure 3.   SmartLM implementation of WSAG4J engine

As we have exactly one template, we only need one agreement factory action (see Figure3). To get the template, negotiate the template and to create agreements, this agreement factory action provides the WSAG4J server actions:

GetLicenseTemplateAction implements GetTemplateAction to retrieve a license template.

NegotiateLicenseTemplateAction implements NegotiateAction to negotiate the variables of a license template according to the creation constraints before creating an agreement.

CreateLicenseAgreementAction implements CreateAgreementAction to finally create the agreement, which is based on the initial template and is valid against all creation constraints specified in the initial template.

In the following sections, the complete SLA lifecycle is described in detail, starting with describing an agreement template containing licenses and how it is created, and going on with the complete negotiation process further describing agreement creation and ending with agreement termination.

5.3   Creation of license agreement templates

In order to retrieve an agreement template the GetLicenseTemplateAction is invoked. An agreement template is created that is uniquely identified by its name and its id. Also the context of the template contains the name and id of the template. This is required in order to lookup the template instance used to create an agreement offer later on.

Creation constraints are added to depict the structure an agreement offer must have. This allows (i) the client to create an appropriate agreement offer the server may accept and (ii) the server to efficiently validate the offer.

In Figure 4 the structure of an agreement template structure is depicted. The template is composed of the template name, its context, service description terms (SDTs) and creation constraints.

Figure 4.   Structure of a SmartLM license agreement template following the WS-Agreement specification

The template can be seen as a form, which can be filled out by the user to describe the application he wants to use. The service description term "LicenseDescription" uses a newly developed language to describe this license.

5.4   Negotiation

As written in Section 4, the GRAAP group in OGF provides an extension of WS-Agreement specification to support multi-round negotiation in addition to the existing simple offer-accept/reject protocol. This extension is implemented in WSAG4J and used in SmartLM to negotiate the terms of license usage. The negotiation step is optional and can be skipped. Therefore, the client is also allowed to directly create an agreement offer as described in Section 5.5.

After retrieving a license template from the server, the user can fill out the template with regards to its needs. It is expected that the user knows which application he wants to execute and that he is able to set the application name and its version and also the features of an application. This information could e.g. be provided by the ISV of the application the user intends to execute. Nevertheless it is also possible for the user to provide only the application name and he will get back a license description which holds all details of this application. To do so, it is necessary to specify a negotiation goal in the second license description term (NegotiationGoal) of the template. Default negotiation goal is "TIMESLOT". This tells the server that the user wants to get a free timeslot for his selected features and values. Another negotiation goal is "FEATURES" which tells the server, that he needs to provide all features with maximum values of an application. The application name can be a regular expression and it is possible that there are several licenses which fulfill the request (e.g. several versions of the application are available). In this case the returned template contains several service description terms comprising a license description. The user then needs to choose the right one from this licenses.

When the user filled in the template, the client creates a NegotiationQuote and sends it to the SLA and Negotiation Service (AgreementProvider). The quote has the same structure as an agreement and is also based on the initial template which is identified by the template id and name contained in the context of the quote.

At this point the NegotiateLicenseAction is invoked, trying to create a suitable template based on the quote. The license management service is queried to find a suitable license and in case of "TIMESLOT" negotiation goal, also a suitable timeslot for the requested application. The accounting and billing service is queried to find out how much the execution of this application will cost. If all requirements are fulfilled, a new Template is created and returned to the client. Now the template is filled with a valid license description.

If this template suits the user, he will create an AgreementOffer and the negotiation process is successfully completed. Otherwise the user may quit the process, or try to further negotiate the template until the server can provide a suitable template.

5.5   Agreement creation

The CreateLicenseAgreementAction is associated with the previously defined license agreement template. It is invoked, when a valid agreement offer was received. The template used to create an offer is identified by the template name and id contained in the context of an agreement offer. Before the CreateLicenseAgreementAction is invoked, the WSAG4J engine validates the agreement offer against its creation constraints. And only if the offer is valid, the CreateLicenseAgreementAction is invoked.

During invocation, the following actions will be accomplished:

Check policies The policy engine is queried to check if the user meets all conditions to use the license.

License reservation If all creation constraints are fulfilled, the license service is called in order to confirm the reservation of the license. Each consumable feature will be blocked during the negotiated time frame.

Token creation Only when all features of the license were scheduled successfully, the license service creates a license token. This token is used later on to run the Application.

Usage record creation An initial usage record describing the reserved license is created to keep track of license usage. This record is sent to the Usage Record Service, which notifies the Accounting and Billing system and provides it upon request to the Accounting and Billing system.

Persistent storage of SLAs To make SLAs persistent and reliable they are stored in the SmartLM Storage Service, which is responsible for storing data permanently. In case of a system crash, the SLAs can be recovered without losing any data

5.6 Agreement termination

If the user needs to terminate the agreement unexpectedly before the agreement ends automatically, the following actions are performed: The license service is called to cancel the reservation. He frees the reserved license features and invalidates the license token. The Policy Engine is queried if the user has to pay for the entire reservation or whether he is charged only what he used until cancellation. If the user is only charged for the real license usage, the accounting and billing system is queried to calculate the new price and a new Usage Record is created holding the real license usage and the actual price.

6. Conclusions

We presented the first implementation of WS-Agreement-Negotiation, which extends WS-Agreement allowing more sophisticated multi-round negotiations between the service consumer and the service provider about the QoS of the requested service. WS-Agreement-Negotiation has been realized by the SmartLM project where it is used to negotiate the license terms and their temporal availability when the user requests a license from the license management service. Additionally, WS-Agreement-Negotiation might also be used during run-time of the application when it turns out, that the terms of the license need to be modified. One major objective of this implementation was to provide a negotiation protocol that does not break the existing WS-Agreement 1.0 protocol or renders the schema of the templates incompatible with previous versions.

In the background of this implementation SmartLM was closely cooperating with the GRAAP-WG of the Open Grid Forum where the specification of a negotiation protocol has been discussed and prepared over the last two years. Jointly with the GRAAP-WG we created with this implementation the basis for the specification of WS-Agreement-Negotiation that is currently prepared by the GRAAP-WG to be submitted to the OGF editor as a proposed recommendation.

Besides the definition of the WS-Agreement-Negotiation specification we focus our future work on the re-negotiation of SLAs already in force. This work will also be driven by use-cases from the SmartLM project. In general the problem we address is the following: After the initial negotiation of the terms of a SLA, once the SLA is in force, it may happen that one of the agreement parties needs to change the agreement for some reason. For example, the provider receives a request for a service from a customer with a higher priority and this request can only be fulfilled when modifying active agreements. Or, the customer wants to extend the time he can use a certain service or increase the resources for this service because it became obvious that obtaining tangible results need more time or resources. Or, the other way round the results delivered by the service are corrupt and the customer is interested to cancel the SLA. In all of these cases the parties would benefit from the possibility to enter a further negotiation phase for re-negotiating the SLA.

The GRAAP-WG already discussed several approaches for the re-negotiation of SLAs. Again, as a precondition it was decided that WS-Agreement should not be modified in an incompatible way when re-negotiation is introduced. There are a number of boundary conditions, one of them being the fact, that the original agreement keeps in force until it is superseded by a new one through the re-negotiation process. This guarantees that whenever the re-negotiation process fails or is aborted by one of the parties the original agreement binding both parties is still in force.

Acknowledgments

Some of the work reported in this paper has been funded by the European Commissions ICT programme in the FP7 project SmartLM under grant #216759. Most of the parts dealing with WS-Agreement and WS-Agreement-Negotiation directly stem from the work of the GRAAP-WG of the Open Grid Forum. In particular many discussions of SLA negotiation in the GRAAP-WG finally led to the draft specification, which has been implemented in SmartLM.

References

[1] F.M.T. Brazier, D.G.A. Mobach, and B.J. Overeinder. A WS-Agreement Based Resource Negotiation Framework for Mobile Agents. In Scalable Computing Practice and Experience, Vol. 7(1), Warsaw School of Social Psychology, Poland, pages 23–36, March 2006.

[2] G. Di Modica, V. Regalbuto, O. Tomarchio, and L. Vita. Enabling re-negotiations of SLA by extending the WS-Agreement specification. In IEEE International Conference on Services Computing 2007 (SCC 2007), pages 248–251, July 2007.

[3] P. Hasselmeyer, H. Mersch, H.-N. Quyen, L. Schubert, B. Koller, and Ph. Wieder. Implementing an SLA Negotiation Framework. Expanding the Knowledge Economy: Issues, Applications, Case Studies, pages 154–161, 2007. ISBN: 978-1-58603-801-4.

[4] S. Hudert, H. Ludwig, and G. Wirtz. Negotiating Service Levels – A generic negotiation framework for WS-Agreement. In Proceedings of the 20th International Conference on Software Engineering and Knowledge Engineering, 2008. to appear.

[5] M. Parkin, P. Hasselmeyer, B. Koller, and P. Wieder. An SLA Re-negotiation Protocol. In Proceedings of the 2nd Non Functional Properties and Service Level Agreements in Service Oriented Computing Workshop (NFPSLA-SOC'08) in conjunction with the 6th IEEE European Conference on Web Services, Springer, 2008. to appear.

[6] M. Parkin, R.M. Badia, and J. Martrat. A Comparison of SLA Use in Six of the European Commissions FP6 Projects. Technical Report TR-0129, Institute on Resource Management and Scheduling, CoreGRID - Network of Excellence, April 2008.

[7] Ph. Wieder, O. Wäldrich, and W. Ziegler. A meta-scheduling service for co-allocating arbitrary types of resources. In Proceedings of the 6th International Conference, Parallel Processing and Applied Mathematics, PPAM 2005, LNCS, Vol. 3911, Poznan, Poland, pages 782–791, Springer, September 2005.

[8] PHOSPHORUS – Lambda User Controlled Infrastructure for European Research, 2009. http://www.ist-phosphorus.eu/.

[9] A. Pichot, Ph. Wieder, O. Wäldrich, and W. Ziegler. Towards dynamic Service Level Agreement negotiation - an approach based on WS-Agreement". In Web information systems and technologies, LNBIP, pages 107–119. Springer, 2009.

[10] C. Qu, L. Schubert, B. Koller, and Ph. Wieder. Towards Autonomous Brokered SLA Negotiation. In Proceedings of the eChallenges Conference (e-2006), October 2006.

[11] J. Seidel, O. Wäldrich, Ph. Wieder, R. Yahyapour, and W. Ziegler. SLA for Resource Management and Scheduling - A Survey. In Grid Middleware and Services: Challenges and Solutions, CoreGRID series 8, Springer, 2008.

[12] SmartLM – Grid-friendly software licensing for location independent application execution, 2009. http://www.smartlm.eu/.

[13] Web Service Agreement (WS-Agreement). Grid Forum Document, GFD.107, proposed recommendation, Open Grid Forum. URL: http://www.ogf.org/documents/GFD.107.pdf.

[14] W. Ziegler, Ph. Wieder, and D. Battré. Extending WS-Agreement for dynamic negotiation of Service Level Agreements. Technical Report TR-0172, Institute on Resource Management and Scheduling, CoreGRID - Network of Excellence, August 2008.

ENABLING OPEN CLOUD MARKETS THROUGH WS-AGREEMENT EXTENSIONS

Marcel Risch, Jörn Altmann
Seoul National University, San 56-1, Sillim-Dong, Gwanak-Gu, Seoul, 151-742, South-Korea
marcel.risch@temep.snu.ac.kr
jorn.altmann@acm.org

Abstract   Research into computing resource markets has mainly considered the question of which market mechanisms provide a fair resource allocation. However, while developing such markets, the definition of the unit of trade (i.e. the definition of resource) has not been given much attention. In this paper, we analyze the requirements for tradable resource goods. Based on the results, we suggest a detailed goods definition, which is easy to understand, can be used with many market mechanisms, and addresses the needs of a Cloud resource market. The goods definition captures the complete system resource, including hardware specifications, software specifications, the terms of use, and a pricing function. To demonstrate the usefulness of such a standardized goods definition, we demonstrate its application in the form of a WS-Agreement template for a number of market mechanisms for commodity system resources.

Keywords: Grid economics, unit of trade, system resource trading, Cloud computing market, system virtualization, contract templates, WS-agreements, service level contract, Cloud economics.

P. Wieder et al. (eds.), *Grids and Service-Oriented Architectures for Service Level Agreements,*
DOI 10.1007/978-1-4419-7320-7_10, © Springer Science+Business Media, LLC 2010

1.   Introduction

There have been many proposals for Grid markets, such as Spawn [1], Tycoon [2], GRACE [3], GridEcon [4], and MACE [5]. The main goal of these projects was to develop a market mechanism, which would allow for an efficient and fair allocation of computing resources. To achieve this goal, some projects have decided to focus on the most important aspect of a computing resource: its computational power.

These simplifications were acceptable since some applications predominantly require computing power. Furthermore, since designing a market mechanism for complex goods is difficult, initial simplifications had to be made for implementing a proof-of-concept. However, since the development of computing resource markets has progressed and a number of commercial offerings are now available, these simplifications must be removed and the tradable good must be described in its entirety to ensure that traders in a computing resource market can describe their offers and demands accurately. In this paper, we propose a detailed definition of a general scheme for defining computing resources (i.e. units of trade) that consists not only of the hardware but also of software and the terms of use. A complete resource contract, which can also be called Service Level Agreement, contains the definition of system resources, the software purchased with it (if applicable), the pricing function, and the guarantees given by the provider. Such a contract would capture all aspects that are relevant to trading of Cloud resources.

Traditionally, the guarantees given by the provider and the duties of both providers and buyers have been captured by Service Level Agreements (SLAs). While many works on computing resource markets assume the existence of Service Level Agreements [6–7], there is very little work on the exact definition of a SLA for resources. The best attempt has been made by the OGF GRAAP working group [8], which provided the WS-Agreement scheme [9]. However, this scheme is not aimed at system resources in particular but rather at general services. We will demonstrate how WS-Agreement can be used as a basis for developing a Computing Resource Definition Language (CRDL), which can be used in the setting of computing resource markets. Finally, we show how this new WS-Agreement extension can be used in a number of different market mechanisms and show that such a resource description will simplify resource trading.

2.   State of the Art

2.1   WS-Agreement

WS-Agreement was developed to allow service consumers and service providers to form contracts which specify the service details, the guarantees, the obligations, and the penalties for each party concerned. This is, of course, exactly what is needed in Cloud computing markets, since Cloud computing resources are services.

WS-Agreement comprises three major sections: Name, Context, and Terms. The Name section contains the optional name of the agreement and a unique ID. In the Context section, information about the service provider and consumer are noted, as well as the expiration time of the agreement. The Terms section contains information about the service terms and the guarantees. The service terms describe the service in as much detail as possible, while the guarantees describe which minimum performance the service will provide.

In general, WS-Agreement can be used to describe services of any kind. At the same time, it also implements a negotiation model for negotiating an agreement. This versatility should make WS-Agreement a very useful tool in open Cloud markets. However, the fact that WS-Agreement is not intended to be specific to any type of market makes it very difficult to use for computing services. We therefore will use the basic structure of WS-Agreement to develop a Computing Resource Definition Language (CRDL), which can be used in Cloud computing markets.

2.2   Existing Commercial Cloud Offers

In recent years, a large number of commercial Cloud providers have entered the utility computing market, using virtualization. Now, there are a number of different types of services which are sold under the label of "Cloud Computing". On the one hand, there are resource providers, such as Amazon (e.g. EC2 [10]) and Tsunamic Technologies [11], who provide computing resources. On the other hand, there are providers, who not only sell their own computing resources but also their own software services, such as Google Apps [12]and Salesforce.com [13]. Furthermore, there are companies that attempt to run a mixed approach, i.e. they allow users to create their own software services but, at the same time, the company offers various support services (i.e. platform services) to its customers. An example of such an approach is the Sun N1 Grid [14].

Looking at these resource providers, it should be noted that none of them use WS-Agreement to describe the SLAs. Instead, some of these providers use their legal staff to draft the SLA in human-readable format [15]. Others, such as Sun and Tsunamic Technologies, do not even provide SLAs publicly. The fact that these providers do not use WS-Agreement for their SLAs indicates that WS-Agreement still has some major shortcomings.

2.3   Open Cloud Market Enablers

In addition to the introduction of virtualization in data centers, several companies (e.g. Enomaly [16]or Fluid Operations [17]) now offer platforms to integrate in-house resources with externally purchased Cloud resources. These products not only allow users to turn their data center into a Cloud but also allow users to act as providers for resource services. Using such software, data center operators could easily be encouraged to participate in an open Cloud market, since the integration of internal and external resources is simplified.

A company that follows this idea is Zimory [18]. Its product turns a regular data center into an intra-company Cloud, allowing an efficient use of resources. In addition, Zimory also allows its costumers to sell spare capacity via its own marketplace. During times of high demand, of course, resources can then be purchased via the Zimory Cloud.

At this time, none of these companies seem to offer the capability to use any kind of SLAs with their services. However, if an open Cloud market were to be established, provisions for legally binding contracts would have to be made. Since WS-Agreement already uses a very clear structure, this template could be adapted to be more suitable for Cloud resources.

2.4   Computing Resource Markets Research

The research into system resource markets can be divided into two groups, when looking at their description of tradable goods. The first group does not define goods at all, while the second group focuses on one aspect of a computing resource only.

The first group consists to a large extend of early Grid market designs. Examples for these early designs are GRACE and designs by Buyya [19]. In these early designs, the analysis of Grid market entities and the architecture of such a market have been analyzed. However, the good "computing resource" has not been defined. Since the tradable good has not been considered, the question of how the contractual obligations can be defined has also not been addressed.

The second group of Grid market research has simplified the computing resource good. The MACE exchange takes a small step away from the initial market architectures [5]. The authors recognize the importance of developing a definition for the tradable good. However, they abstract computing resources into services that can be traded; the actual definition has never been supplied.

Another approach, which was taken by several research groups, was the focus on computing power, either in the form of Java OPerations (JOPs) within the Popcorn market [20], or in the form of CPU slices within the Spawn market [1]. These goods are very restrictive, since they require detailed knowledge about the factors (e.g. application requirements, the compiler vendor, the instruction sets of the CPU) that influence the amount of computing power needed.

Lastly, there is the Tycoon market [2], which was developed before virtualization tools (e.g. Xen [21]) became widely used. The initial stages worked with basic computing cycles and it was planned to extend this market by making use of virtualization. However, it seems that the effort has been discontinued.

Overall, much of the resource market research has worked with either simplified definitions of the tradable good or without defining the good at all. Therefore, since Grid research did not provide any foundation for defining a computing resource good, we will use WS-Agreement to develop such a definition. WS-Agreement was chosen for its flexibility: it will be used as a basis for developing a Computing Resource Definition Language, keeping the structure of WS-Agreement but expanding it to describe resources in detail. The usefulness of WS-Agreement for defining extensions has been shown quite frequently [22–24].

3. Extending WS-Agreement

3.1 Diversity of Goods

In an open market environment, diverse computing resources have to be described in a common format so that customers can determine the differences between various resource offers. This diversity may seem daunting at first but it should be remembered that trading diverse resources is already possible in practice for other goods. Looking at the Chicago Mercantile Exchange (CME) [25], we can see that even diverse products such as live cattle can be traded. Since live animals are extremely diverse, the trading contracts are very detailed, including penalties and obligations, as the following example shows:

"A par delivery unit is 40,000 pounds of USDA estimated Yield Grade 3, 55% Choice, 45% Select quality grade live steers, averaging between 1,100 pounds and 1,425 pounds with no individual steer weighing more than 100 pounds above or below the average weight for the unit. No individual animal weighing less than 1,050 pounds or more than 1,475 pounds shall be deliverable. Par delivery units shall have an estimated average hot yield of 63%. [...] Steers weighing from 100 to 200 pounds over or under the average weight of the steers in the delivery unit shall be deliverable at a discount of 3c per pound, provided that no individual animal weighing less than 1,050 or more than 1,475 pounds shall be deliverable." (pg. 3, [26])

This principle of a complete contract should be adopted for infrastructure markets so that all parties (buyers and sellers) involved in the trade can easily understand the properties of the traded good and have a common reference to the traded resource.

3.2   Composition of the Service Level Contract

The benefits of using WS-Agreement to compose Service Level Contracts lies in the fact that WS-Agreement already comprises all categories necessary for describing a computing resource definition. Therefore, all that has to be done is to extend WS-Agreement in such a way that it becomes more specific. All excerpts from WS-Agreement in this chapter have been taken from [27]. The basic structure of WS-Agreement consists of a Name, an AgreementContext, and a Terms section. In a market environment, in which the resource definitions are managed centrally, the agreement name will be specified in advance. The agreement ID will only be created when a buyer and seller decide to trade resources.

3.2.1   Agreement Context.   The AgreementContext section contains information about the service provider and the agreement initiators and respondents. The full specification of the AgreementContext section is shown below (note, all extensions to the WS-Agreement that we suggest are indicated in italic throughout the remainder of the paper):

```
<wsag:Context xs:anyAttribute>
    <wsag:AgreementInitiator>xs:anyType</wsag:AgreementInitiator> ?
    <wsag:AgreementResponder>xs:anyType</wsag:AgreementResponder> ?
    <wsag:ServiceConsumer>wsag:AgreementRoleType</
    wsag:ServiceConsumer>
    <wsag:ServiceProvider>wsag:AgreementRoleType</
    wsag:ServiceProvider>
    <wsag:StartingTime>xs:DateTime</wsag:StartingTime>
    <wsag:EndingTime>xs:DateTime</wsag:EndingTime>
    <wsag:PurchaseTime>xs:DateTime</wsag:PurchaseTime>
    <wsag:ExpirationTime>xs:DateTime</wsag:ExpirationTime>
    <wsag:TemplateId>xs:string</wsag:TemplateId> ?
    <wsag:TemplateName>xs:string</wsag:TemplateName> ?
    <xs:any/> *
</wsag:Context>
```

Figure 1.   General Structure of WS-Agreement.

The AgreementInitiator and AgreementResponder sections will have to be filled according to the market mechanism, but can be left blank if they are not needed. The Service Provider section, as well as the newly created ServiceConsumer section, will be filled with information about the service provider and the service consumer, respectively. Both fields are mandatory.

The StartingTime section allows for future delivery of the service. Since even spot market sales have a lag time, which allows the provider to set up the resources, this starting time is vital to ensure that the agreement covers the relevant time schemes. We also introduced an EndingTime section, which denotes the time at which the resources revert to their owner. Both these fields are obligatory. The PurchaseTime section describes the time of purchase of the SLA. This is necessary for some pricing function as explained in section 3.2.4.

The ExpirationTime section will be filled in according to the expiration time of the contract. This time must be at least the same time as the ending time to ensure that the contract is valid for the entire duration of the resource usage. The TemplateID and TemplateName sections will be filled as needed.

3.2.2   Terms.   The Terms section defines both the service that is traded, as well as the guarantees that the provider is willing to make. Furthermore, this section can contain a description of the penalties as well as a description of the restrictions. The Terms section contains elements for the service description, service reference, service properties, and the guarantee terms.

For computing resources, the ServiceDescriptionTerm section can be used to describe the physical resource with respect to CPU, main memory, hard disk, and the network. A detailed description of a resource is shown below on the left.

Figure 2.   ServiceDescriptionTerm and processor definition.

Most of these complex types will have to be expanded. On the right-hand side of Figure 2, we demonstrate how the processor can be described in detail. In Figure 3, we show how the network access and the software parameters can be described.

```
<xs:element name="Network">
  <xs:complexType>
    <xs:sequence>
      <wsag:ExactlyOne>
        <xs:element
        name="MaximumTransmissionSpeedMbitPe
        rSec" type="xs:decimal"/>
        <xs:element name="CacheSizeMB"
        type="xs:decimal"/>
      </wsag:ExactlyOne>
    </xs:sequence>
  </xs:complexType>
</xs:element>
```

```
<xs:element name="Software">
  <xs:complexType>
    <xs:sequence>
      <wsag:ExactlyOne>
        <xs:element
        name="VirtualizationSoftware"
        type="xs:string"/>
        <xs:element name="OperatingSystems"
        type="xs:string"/>
        <xs:element name="StaticIP"
        type="xs:boolean"/>
      </wsag:ExactlyOne>
    </xs:sequence>
  </xs:complexType>
</xs:element>
```

Figure 3.   Description of network and software.

On the left side of Figure 4, the main memory is specified; on the right side, the hard disk can be specified.

```
<xs:element name="MainMemory">
  <xs:complexType>                              <xs:element name="HDD">
    <xs:sequence>                                 <xs:complexType>
      <wsag:ExactlyOne>                             <xs:sequence>
        <xs:element name="Type"                       <wsag:ExactlyOne>
        type="xs:string"/>                              <xs:element name="SizeGB"
        <xs:element name="SizeGB"                       type="xs:decimal"/>
        type="xs:decimal"/>                             <xs:element name="RPM"
        <xs:element name="MemoryClockMHz"               type="xs:integer"/>
        type="xs:integer"/>                             <xs:element name="SeekTimeMS"
        <xs:element name="CycleTimeNs"                  type="xs:decimal"/>
        type="xs:integer"/>                             <xs:element
        <xs:element name="IOBusClockMHz"                name="DataTransferRateMbitPerSec"
        type="xs:integer"/>                             type="xs:decimal"/>
        <xs:element                                     <xs:element name="CacheSizeMB"
        name="DataTransferMBitPerSecond"                type="xs:decimal"/>
        type="xs:integer"/>                           </wsag:ExactlyOne>
      </wsag:ExactlyOne>                             </xs:sequence>
    </xs:sequence>                                 </xs:complexType>
  </xs:complexType>                             </xs:element>
</xs:element>
```

Figure 4.   Description of memory and hard disk.

The software section describes whether a virtualization tool was used to create the resource, and if so, which types of software containers can be run on the resource. This allows the user to determine whether this resource is capable of running software containers already owned by the user, or if new containers have to be created. Furthermore, if the provider desires, this category can also describe which operating systems can run on the resource or is pre-installed. This is especially important if virtualization tools are used, since these tools place some restrictions on the operating systems that can be deployed. In addition, this category can describe whether static or dynamic IP addresses are used.

3.2.3   Guarantee Terms.   The GuaranteeTerms section describes the guarantees the service provider will have to give. In the case of computing resources, the resource description given in the ServiceDescription section is a minimum performance that must be provided. To see how the WS-Agreement GuaranteeTerms can be extended, we will have to look at this section in more detail. The GuaranteeTerms consists of the ServiceScope section, the Qualifying-Condition section, the ServiceLevelObjective section and the BusinessValueList section.

The ServiceScope describes to which element of the service term the guarantee applies (e.g. for software services, one element could be the response time). In the case of computing resources, the guarantees cover all parameters of the computing resource as a whole. The QualifyingCondition section describes when a guarantee starts to apply. In the case of computing resources, this is the moment when the user is given control of the resource. The ServiceLevel-Objectives section describes when a guarantee is considered to be met. In the case of computing resources, this is the case if the resource is available for the specified amount of time and if all parameters in the description are met, e.g. the processor speed is correct and memory size is correct.

The BusinessValueList section describes penalties and rewards. It consists of the Importance, Penalty, Reward, Preference and CustomBusinesValue sections. The Importance section describes the importance of a given business value. This can be filled in, if the providers or consumers so desire.

The Rewards section describes the reward that could be incurred for meeting an objective. In the case of computing resources, this could be the price that has to be paid by the consumer for using the specified resource. The Preference

```
<wsag:Reward>
  <xs:element name="Price">
    <xs:complexType>
      <xs:sequence>
        <xs:element name="One_Time_Fee"
          type="xs:decimal"/>
        <xs:element name="CPU_HR"
          type="xs:decimal"/>
        <xs:element name="Upload"
          type="xs:decimal"/>
        <xs:element name="Download"
          type="xs:decimal"/>
        <xs:element name="Storage"
          type="xs:decimal"/>
      </xs:sequence>
    </xs:complexType>
  </xs:element>
</wsag:Reward>
```

```
<wsag:Preference>
  <xs:element name="PriceValidity">
    <xs:complexType>
      <xs:sequence>
        <xs:element name="BusinessValueListReference"
          type="wsag:BusinessValueListID"/>
        <xs:element name="CPU_HR_Lower_Usage_Bound" type="xs:decimal"/>
        <xs:element name="CPU_HR_Upper_Usage_Bound" type="xs:decimal"/>
        <xs:element name="CPU_HR_Min_Usage" type="xs:decimal"/>
        <xs:element name="Upload_Lower_Usage_Bound" type="xs:decimal"/>
        <xs:element name="Upload_Upper_Usage_Bound" type="xs:decimal"/>
        <xs:element name="Upload_Min_Usage" type="xs:decimal"/>
        <xs:element name="Download_Lower_Usage_Bound" type="xs:decimal"/>
        <xs:element name="Download_Upper_Usage_Bound" type="xs:decimal"/>
        <xs:element name="Download_Min_Usage" type="xs:decimal"/>
        <xs:element name="Storage_Lower_Usage_Bound" type="xs:decimal"/>
        <xs:element name="Storage_Upper_Usage_Bound" type="xs:decimal"/>
        <xs:element name="Storage_Min_Usage" type="xs:decimal"/>
        <wsag:StartingTime>xs:DateTime</wsag:StartingTime>
        <wsag:EndingTime>xs:DateTime</wsag:EndingTime>
        <xs:element name="Min_Usage_Time_Minutes" type="xs:decimal"/>
      </xs:sequence>
    </xs:complexType>
  </xs:element>
</wsag:Preference>
```

Figure 5.   Reward and Preference sections.

section is used in cases where multiple business values apply to the service at the same time. In such a case, the preference indicates which business value should be used. In the case of computing resources, this section expresses pricing and multiple pricing models can be ranked according to their preference. This allows for different pricing models to be applied to different usage and quality levels. Note, if multiple prices apply for the same usage, the consumer will have to pay all fees.

The Penalty section describes the obligations of consumers and providers. In this case, consumers and providers can be held accountable, if certain conditions are not met. In the case of computing resources, these conditions can be quite diverse, ranging from limiting usage of hardware to excluding certain hardware infrastructures entirely from some customers. The definition of the Penalty section follows the one of the Reward section and uses the structure of the Preference section. If a Reward section and a Penalty section exist with the service level contract, two BusinessValueList sections have to be filled out.

The CustomBusinessValues section can be used to describe usage restrictions and responsibilities of the consumer. These are vital to the contract, since many aspects of the resource usage can be affected by these rules.

4.   CRDL in Different Market Mechanisms

The BusinessValueList section describes penalties and rewards. It consists of the Importance, Penalty, Reward, Preference and CustomBusinesValue sections. The Importance section describes the importance of a given business value. This can be filled in, if the providers or consumers so desire.

4.1   Posted Price

In a posted price market, providers are free to create any resource types, which they deem to be tradable. These freely created resource types can also come with highly individualized Terms of Use. For the Computing Resource Definition Language, this means that the Terms section would, in all likelihood, be different for different providers. However, in order to achieve understandability, the Terms would link to an external reference, where the Terms are written in natural language and can be seen by consumers.

In a posted price market environment, the offers could be centrally listed and potential customers can then search these offers based on their unit-of-trade requirements. Such matching procedures have been proposed in [28]. Using the CRDL, this search procedure will be simplified, since the vital parameters can be easily compared.

4.2   Negotiation Environment

In a negotiation process, a provider and consumer can negotiate the different categories of the computing resource contract individually. Should the need arise, both parties can even negotiate the individual aspects of each of the four contract categories. In this case, the contract template helps both parties to structure their negotiation process.

Therefore, the CRDL does not hinder the bargaining partners to negotiate each aspect of a resource. Instead it simplifies the procedure if both parties can agree on standard components. In fact, any mix of standard and individualized components can be combined to form a new contract. Further simplifications are achieved by the fact that WS-Agreement already includes some tools for negotiations which can be used by the trading parties. Furthermore, the flexible pricing section allows both parties to define different prices for individual components. This will ensure that the negotiating parties can be certain that their pricing requirements are met.

4.3   Single Auction

In a single auction, the provider simply posts the service level contract without setting the price of the good. The resource consumer searches for suitable resources being currently auctioned and bids for resources using his bidding strategy. Depending on the auction, the consumer bids for the good and, if he wins, gives the purchase price to the auctioneer. The final service level agreement comprises the service level contract filled with the price associated with the winning bid of the consumer.

The advantage of using CRDL contracts lies in the easy-to-understand description of the traded good. The consumer can easily determine which capabilities each resource has and what the provider is willing to guarantee. Furthermore, since the good is fully described and perhaps only the price is missing, the auction procedure does not need to be adapted to be able to work with other goods of this type of good. Therefore, any existing auction market can work with CRDL. The bid would be a simple value pair <contract ID, price>.

4.4 Discussion of the Computing Resource Definition Language

All market mechanisms use the same template to define the tradable good, i.e. the computing resource. While some market mechanisms, such as single auctions, require such a stringent structure, others are more lenient. Since WS-Agreement is used as a basis, traders will easily understand the structure. Furthermore, if the restrictions, penalties and responsibilities are defined in legal terms, the existing template can then be taken to court.

The comparability requirement of different Computing Resource Contracts is provided not only through a standard format, but also through the same structure of all contracts. This means that the important aspects of each contract can be easily found and can then be compared. However, this requires additional effort in standardizing SLAs, which has been started within the SLA framework of OGF [9].

The flexibility of CRDL is given by the fact that it can represent a large number of different resources types. This structure of a contract allows for individual parts to be, to some extent, standardized. The individual parts can still be combined in many ways to form contracts.

Since CRDL allows a wide array of resources to be described and resource descriptions with CRDL are understandable by all parties, comparisons of units of trades will be simple. Therefore, it is likely that the resource descriptions with CRDL will be accepted by a large number of users.

5. Conclusion and Future Work

In this paper, we have introduced the Computing Resource Definition Language (CRDL), an extension to WS-Agreement. It is aimed at capturing the complexity of system resources in a single descriptor, which can be traded in many market environments. The usefulness of this extension has been discussed by showing its application to different market mechanisms. The main goal was to enhance the usefulness of WS-Agreement for markets where many different market mechanisms can exist. In particular, we showed how CRDL can be applied to utility computing markets for virtualized goods.

References

[1] C.A. Waldspurger, T. Hogg, B.A. Huberman, J.O. Kephart, W.S. Stornetta. Spawn: A Distributed Computational Economy. IEEE Transactions on Software Engineering, 18(2):103–117, Februar 1992.

[2] K. Lai, L. Rasmusson, E. Adar, L. Zhang, and B.A. Huberman. Tycoon: An implementation of a distributed, market-based resource allocation system. Multiagent Grid Syst. 1(3):169–182, August 2005.

[3] R. Buyya, D. Abramson, and J. Giddy. An economy grid architecture for service-oriented grid computing. 10th IEEE International Heterogeneous Computing Workshop (HCW 2001), San Francisco, CA, IEEE Computer Society Press: Los Alamitos, April 2001.

[4] J. Altmann, C. Courcoubetis, M. Dramitinos, G.D. Stamoulis, T. Rayna, M. Risch, C. Bannink. A Market Place for Computing Resources. GECON 2008, Workshop on Grid Economics and Business Models, Las Palmas, Spain, LNCS, Springer, August 2008.

[5] B. Schnizler, D. Neumann, D. Veit, C. Weinhardt. Trading Grid Services - A Multi-attribute Combinatorial Approach. European Journal of Operational Research, 187(3):943–961, 2008.

[6] M. Macias, G. Smith, O.F. Rana, J. Guitart, J. Torres. Enforcing Service Level Agreements using an Economically Enhanced Resource Manager. In: Workshop on Economic Models and Algorithms for Grid Systems (EMAGS 2007), Texas, USA, 2007.

[7] A. Sahai, S. Graupner, V. Machiraju, and A. Moorsel. Specifying and Monitoring Guarantees in Commercial Grids through SLA. In Proceedings of the 3rd international Symposium on Cluster Computing and the Grid (May 12 - 15, 2003). CCGRID. IEEE Computer Society, Washington, DC, 2003.

[8] The Open Grid Forum (OGF), http://www.ogf.org/, 2008.

[9] A. Andrieux, K. Czajkowski, A. Dan, K. Keahey, H. Ludwig, T. Nakata, J. Pruyne, J. Rofrano, S. Tuecke, and M. Xu. Web Services Agreement Specification (WS-Agreement). GWD-R (Proposed Recommendation), Open Grid Forum, 2007.

[10] Amazon Elastic Compute Cloud (Amazon EC2), http://aws.amazon.com/ec2/, 2009.

[11] Tsunamic Technologies Inc., http://www.clusterondemand.com/, 2008.

[12] Google Apps, http://www.google.com/apps/, March 2009.

[13] Salesforce.com, http://www.salesforce.com, March 2009.

[14] Sun Grid, http://www.sun.com/service/sungrid/index.jsp, 2008.

[15] Amazon, EC2 SLA, http://aws.amazon.com/ec2-sla/, 2009.

[16] Enomaly, http://www.enomaly.com/, 2008.

[17] fluid Operations, http://www.fluidops.com, 2009.

[18] Zimory, http://www.zimory.com/, 2009.

[19] R. Rajkumar and S. Vazhkudai. Compute Power Market: Towards a Market-Oriented Grid. First IEEE International Symposium on Cluster Computing and the Grid (CCGrid'01), page 574, 2001.

[20] O. Regev and N. Nisan. The POPCORN market-an online market for computational resources. In Proceedings of the First international Conference on information and Computation Economies (Charleston, South Carolina, United States, October 25 - 28, 1998), ICE '98, pages 148–157, ACM, New York, NY, 1998.

[21] XenSource, Inc., http://xen.org/, 2008.

[22] M.A. Oey, R.J. Timmer, D.G. Mobach, B.J. Overeinder, and F.M. Brazier. WS-Agreement based resource negotiation in AgentScape. In Proceedings of the 6th international Joint Conference on Autonomous Agents and Multiagent Systems (Honolulu, Hawaii, May 14 - 18, 2007), AAMAS '07, ACM, New York, NY, 2007.

[23] C. Müller, O. Martín-Díaz, A. Ruiz-Cortés, M. Resinas, and P. Fernandez. Improving Temporal-Awareness of WS-Agreement. In Proceedings of the 5th international Conference on Service-Oriented Computing (Vienna, Austria, September 17 - 20, 2007). B.J. Krämer, K. Lin, and P. Narasimhan, (eds.), LNCS, Vol. 4749, pages 193–206, Springer-Verlag, Berlin, Heidelberg, 2007.

[24] W. Jouve, J. Lancia, C. Consel, and C. Pu. A Multimedia-Specific Approach to WS-Agreement. Fourth IEEE European Conference on Web Services (ECOWS'06), pages 44–52, 2006.

[25] Chicago Mercantile Exchange, http://www.cme.com/, 2008.

[26] CME Rulebook, http://www.cmegroup.com/cmegroup/rulebook/CME/II/100/101/101.pdf, 2008.

[27] A. Andrieux, K. Czajkowski, A. Dan, K. Keahey, H. Ludwig, J. Pruyne, J. Rofrano, S. Tuecke, and M. Xu. Web Services Agreement Specifcation (WS-Agreement), Version 2005/09, http://www.ggf.org.

[28] H.K. Bhargava and A. Bagh. Tarif Structures for Pricing Grid Computing Resources. In Gecon 2006, 2006.

SERVICE MEDIATION AND NEGOTIATION BOOTSTRAPPING AS FIRST ACHIEVEMENTS TOWARDS SELF-ADAPTABLE CLOUD SERVICES

Ivona Brandic, Dejan Music, Schahram Dustdar
Institute of Information Systems, Vienna University of Technology
Argentinierstraße 8, 1040 Vienna, Austria
{ivona,dejan,dustdar}@infosys.tuwien.ac.at

Abstract   Nowadays, novel computing paradigms as for example Cloud Computing are gaining more and more on importance. In case of Cloud Computing users pay for the usage of the computing power provided as a service. Beforehand they can negotiate specific functional and non-functional requirements relevant for the application execution. However, providing computing power as a service bears different research challenges. On one hand dynamic, versatile, and adaptable services are required, which can cope with system failures and environmental changes. On the other hand, human interaction with the system should be minimized. In this chapter we present the first results in establishing adaptable, versatile, and dynamic services considering negotiation bootstrapping and service mediation achieved in context of the Foundations of Self-Governing ICT Infrastructures (FoSII) project. We discuss novel meta-negotiation and SLA mapping solutions for Cloud services bridging the gap between current QoS models and Cloud middleware and representing important prerequisites for the establishment of autonomic Cloud services.

Keywords: Autonomic SLA Management, Meta-Negotiations, SLA Mapping, Negotiation Frameworks, Cloud Computing

P. Wieder et al. (eds.), *Grids and Service-Oriented Architectures for Service Level Agreements,*
DOI 10.1007/978-1-4419-7320-7_11, © Springer Science+Business Media, LLC 2010

1.   Introduction

Service-oriented Architectures (SOA) represent a promising approach for implementing ICT systems [4]. Thereby, software is packaged to services and can be accessed independently of the used programming languages, protocols, and platforms. Despite remarkable adoption of SOA as the key concept for the implementation of ICT systems, the full potential of SOA (e.g., dynamism, adaptivity) is still not exploited [19]. SOA approach and Web service technologies represent large scale abstractions and a candidate concept for the implementation novel computing paradigms where sophisticated scientific applications can be accessed as services over Internet [1, 5] or where massively scalable computing is made available to end users as a service as in case of *Cloud Computing* [10]. In all those approaches the access to computing power is provided as a service.

The key benefits of providing computing power as a service are (a) avoidance of expensive computer systems configured to cope with peak performance, (b) pay-per-use solutions for computing cycles requested on-demand, and (c) avoidance of idle computing resources. The development of novel concepts for dynamic, versatile, and adaptive services represents an open and challenging research issue [16]. Major goal of this chapter is to facilitate service negotiation in heterogeneous Clouds. In order to enable service users to find services which best fit to their needs (considering costs, execution time and other functional and non-functional properties), service users should negotiate and communicate with numerous publicly available services.

Non-functional requirements of a service execution are termed as *Quality of Service (QoS)*, and are expressed and negotiated by means of *Service Level Agreements (SLAs)*. *SLA templates* represent empty SLA documents with all required elements like parties, SLA parameters, metrics and objectives, but without QoS values [12]. However, most existing Cloud frameworks assume that the communication partner knows about the *negotiation protocols* before entering the negotiation and that they have matching *SLA templates*. In commercially used Clouds this is an unrealistic assumption since services are discovered dynamically and on demand. Thus, so-called *meta-negotiations* are required to allow two parties to reach an agreement on what specific negotiation protocols, security standards, and documents to use before starting the actual negotiation. The necessity for SLA mappings can be motivated by differences in terminology for a common attribute such as *price*, which may be defined as *usage price* on one side and *service price* on the other, leading to inconsistencies during the negotiation process.

Thus, we approach the gap between existing QoS methods and Cloud services by proposing an architecture for Cloud service management with components for *meta-negotiations* and *SLA mappings* [9, 8, 7]. Meta-negotiations are defined by means of a *meta-negotiation document* where participating parties may express: the pre-requisites to be satisfied for a negotiation, for example, requirement for a specific authentication method; the supported negotiation protocols and document languages for the specification of SLAs; and conditions for the establishment of an agreement, for example, a required third-party arbitrator. SLA mappings are defined by XSLT[1] documents where inconsistent parts of one document are mapped to another document e.g., from consumer's template to provider's template. Moreover, based on SLA mappings and deployed taxonomies, we eliminate semantic inconsistencies between consumer's and providers SLA template.

2. Related Work

Since there is very little exiting work on self-adaptable Cloud services, we look into existing systems in related areas - in particular into existing Grid systems. Currently, a large body of work exists in the area of Grid service negotiation and SLA-based QoS [20, 11]. Work presented in [22] discusses incorporation of SLA-based resource brokering into existing Grid systems. Glatard et al. discuss a probabilistic model of workflow execution time evaluated in context of EGEE grid infrastructure [13]. Work described in [23] presents an approach for dynamic workflow management and optimization using near-realtime performance with strategies for choosing an optimal service, based on user-specified criteria, from several semantically equivalent Web services. Oldham et al. describe a framework for semantic matching of SLAs based on WSDL-S and OWL [21].

Ardagana et al. [3] present an autonomic Grid architecture with mechanisms to dynamically re-configure service center infrastructures, which is basically exploited to fulfill varying QoS requirements. Work presented in [1] extends the service abstraction in the Open Grid Services Architecture (OGSA) for QoS properties focusing on the application layer. Thereby, a given service may indicate the QoS properties it can offer or it may search for other services based on specified QoS properties. Work presented in [11] proposes a generalized resource management model where resource interactions are mapped onto a well defined set of platform-independent SLAs. The model is based on Service Negotiation and Acquisition Protocol (SNAP) providing the lifetime management SLAs.

Dan et al. [12] present a framework for providing customers of Web services differentiated levels of service through the use of automated management and SLAs. Work described in [15] discusses how semantic technologies may be used by mobile devices which need to locate and select appropriate Grid services

---

[1] XSL Transformations (XSLT) Version 1.0, http://www.w3.org/TR/xslt.html

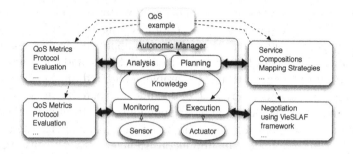

Figure 1.   General Architecture of an Autonomic System Explained on a QoS Example

in an automatic and flexible way. Jurca et al. propose a new form of SLAs where the price is determined by the QoS which is actually delivered by service provider. For the monitoring of QoS a novel approach is introduced based on reputation mechanism [17].

3.   Adaptable, Versatile, and Dynamic services

In this section we discuss how adaptable, versatile, and dynamic services can be realized.

3.1   Overview

To facilitate dynamic, versatile, and adaptive IT infrastructures, SOA systems should react to environmental changes, software failures, and other events which may influence the systems' behavior. Therefore, adaptive systems exploiting self-* properties (self-healing, self-controlling, self-managing, etc.) are needed, where human intervention with the system is minimized. We propose models and concepts for adaptive services building on the approach defined by means of autonomic computing [18, 3].

We identified the following objectives:

Negotiation bootstrapping and service mediation.   The first objective is to facilitate communication between publicly available services. Usually, before service usage, service consumer and service provider have to establish an electronic contract defining terms of use [6, 11]. Thus, they have to negotiate the exact terms of contract (e.g., exact execution time of the service). However, each service provides a unique negotiation protocol often expressed using different languages, representing an obstacle within the SOA architecture. We propose novel concepts for automatic bootstrapping between different protocols and contract formats increasing the number of services a consumer may negotiate with. Consequently, the full potential of public services could be exploited.

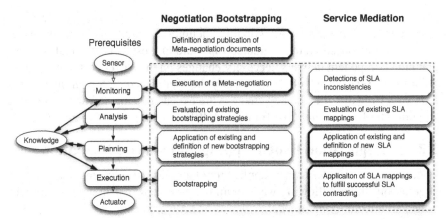

Figure 2. Negotiation Bootstrapping and Service Mediation as Part of the Autonomic Process

Service Enforcement. Services may fail, established contracts between services may be violated. The second objective is to develop methods for service enforcement, where failures and malfunctions are repaired on demand and where services are adapted to changing environmental and system conditions. We propose development of knowledge bases where the directives, policies, and rules for failure adjustment and repair may be specified and stored. Furthermore, adequate methods for the condition specification and condition evaluation are emerging research issues.

Service adaptivity. Service failures or violations of electronic agreements must be detected in an efficient manner. Moreover, the reaction to failures should be done in an adequate way. Thus, the third objective is the development of novel methods for modeling of intelligent logging capabilities at the level of a single service as well as composite services. Sophisticated concepts for the measurement of service execution parameters and Quality of Service (QoS) are needed as well as generic monitoring capabilities which can be customized on-demand for different services.

Service Governance. Policies and rules for service enforcement should not be defined in a static way. Moreover, the rules should evolve over time. The fourth objective is the development of the governing guidelines for rule definition and rule-evolution. This includes the development of adequate languages for rule specification and rule evolution as well as novel reasoning techniques.

In order to achieve aforementioned goals we utilize the principles of *autonomic computing*. Autonomic computing research methodology can be exemplified using Quality of Service (QoS) as shown in Figure 1. The management is done through the following steps: (i) *Monitoring*: QoS managed element is monitored using adequate software sensors; (ii) *Analysis*: The monitored and measured metrics (e.g., execution time, reliability, availability, etc.) are analyzed using knowledge base (condition definition, condition evaluation, etc.); (iii) *Planning*: Based on the evaluated rules and the results of the analysis, the planning component delivers necessary changes on the current setup e.g., renegotiation of services which do not satisfy the established QoS guarantees; (iv) *Execution*: Finally, the planned changes are executed using software actuators and other tools (e.g., *VieSLAF* framework [9]), which query for new services.

3.2   Negotiation Bootstrapping and Service Mediation

Autonomic computing can be applied for other managed elements e.g., service negotiation. In the following we explain the first steps in achieving aforementioned architecture: *meta-negotiations* and *SLA mappings*.

Figure 2 depicts how the principles of autonomic computing can be applied to negotiation bootstrapping and service mediation. As a prerequisite of the negotiation bootstrapping users have to specify a meta-negotiation document describing the requirements of a negotiation, as for example required negotiation protocols, required security infrastructure, provided document specification languages, etc. During the *monitoring phase* all candidate services are selected where negotiation bootstrapping is required. During the *analysis phase* existing knowledge base is queried and potential bootstrapping strategies are found. In case of missing bootstrapping strategies users can define in a semi-automatic way new strategies (*planning phase*). Finally, during the *execution phase* the negotiation is started by utilizing appropriate bootstrapping strategies.

The same procedure can be applied to service mediation. During the service negotiation, inconsistencies in SLA templates may be discovered (*monitoring phase*). During the *analysis phase* existing SLA mappings are analyzed. During the *planning phase* new SLA mappings can be defined, if existing mappings cannot be applied. Finally, during the *execution phase* the newly defined SLA mappings can be applied.

As indicated with bold borders in Figure 2, in this chapter we present solutions for the definition and accomplishment of meta-negotiations (Section 4) and for the specification and applications of SLA mappings (Section 5). In the following section we explain the principles of meta-negotiations.

4.   Meta-Negotiations

In this section, we present an example scenario for the meta-negotiation architecture, and describe the document structure for publishing negotiation details into the meta-negotiation registry.

4.1   Meta-Negotiation Scenario

The meta-negotiation infrastructure can be employed in the following manner: (i) *Publishing*: A service provider publishes descriptions and conditions of supported negotiation protocols into the registry; (ii) *Lookup*: Service consumers perform lookup on the registry database by submitting their own documents describing the negotiations that they are looking for. (iii) *Matching*: The registry discovers service providers who support the negotiation processes that a consumer is interested in and returns the documents published by the service providers; (iv) *Negotiation*: Finally, after an appropriate service provider and a negotiation protocol is selected by a consumer using his/her private selection strategy, negotiations between them may start according to the conditions specified in the provider's document.

In the following we explain the sample meta-negotiation document.

4.2   Meta-Negotiation Document (MND)

The participants publishing into the registry follow a common document structure that makes it easy to discover matching documents. This document structure is presented in Figure 3 and consists of the following main sections.

Each document is enclosed within the `<meta-negotiation>` ... `</meta-negotiation>` tags. Each meta-negotiation (MN) comprises three distinguishing parts, namely *pre-requisites*, *negotiation* and *agreement* as described in the following paragraphs.

Pre-requisites.   The conditions to be satisfied before a negotiation starts are defined within the `<pre-requisite>` element (see Figure 3, lines 3–10). Pre-requisites define the *role* a participating party takes in a negotiation, the *security credentials* and the *negotiation terms*. The `<security>` element specifies the authentication and authorization mechanisms that the party wants to apply before starting the negotiation process. The negotiation terms specify QoS attributes that a party is willing to negotiate and are specified in the `<negotiation-term>` element. For example, in Figure 3, the negotiation terms of the consumer are *beginTime* and *endTime*, and *price* (line 6).

Negotiation.   Details about the negotiation process are defined within the `<negotiation>` element. Each document language is specified within the `<document>` element. In Figure 3, *WSLA* is specified as the supported document language. Additional attributes specify the URI to the API or WSDL for the documents and their versions supported by the consumer. In Figure 3, *AlternateOffers* is specified as the supported negotiation protocol. In addition to the *name*, *version*, and *schema* attributes, the URI to the WSDL or API of the negotiation protocols is specified by the *location* attribute (line 12).

Agreement.   Once the negotiation has concluded and if both parties agree to the terms, then they have to sign an agreement. This agreement may be verified

126   *GRIDS AND SOA FOR SERVICE LEVEL AGREEMENTS*

```
<meta-negotiation ...>
 <pre-requisite>
  <role name="consumer"/>
  <security> <authentication value="GSI" location="uri"/> </security>
  <negotiation-terms>
   <negotiation-term name="beginTime"/> <negotiation-term name="endTime"/>
  </negotiation-terms>
 </pre-requisite>
 <negotiation>
  <document name="WSLA" value="uri" version="1.0"/>
  <protocol name="alternateOffers" schema="uri" version="1.0" location="uri"/>
 </negotiation>
 <agreement> <confirmation name="arbitrationService" value="uri"/> </agreement>
</meta-negotiation>
```

Figure 3.   Example Meta-negotiation Document

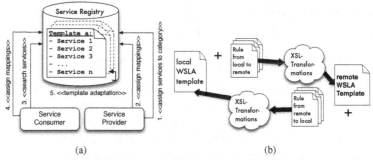

(a)   (b)

Figure 4.   Management of SLA-Mappings (a) Scenario for XSL Transformations (b)

by a third party organization or may be logged with another institution who will also arbitrate in case of a dispute. These modalities are specified within the `<agreement>` clause of the meta-negotiation document as shown in line 14. The meta-negotiation architecture described here was experimentally evaluated and the results were presented in a previous publication [8].

5.   SLA mappings

In the presented approach each SLA template has to be published into a registry where negotiation partners i.e., provider and consumer, can find each other.

5.1   Management of SLA mappings

Figure 4(a) depicts the architecture for the management of SLA mappings and participating parties. The registry comprises different *SLA templates* whereby each of them represent a specific application domain, e.g., SLA templates for medical, telco or life science domain. Thus, each service provider may assign his/her service to a particular template (see step 1 in Figure 4(a)) and afterwards assign SLA mappings if necessary (see step 2). Each template *a* may have *n* services assigned.

Service consumer may search for the services using meta-data and search terms (step 3). After finding appropriate services each service consumer may define mappings to the appropriate template the selected service is assigned to (step 4). Thereafter, the negotiation between service consumer and service provider may start as described in the next section. As already mentioned templates are not defined in a static way. Based on the assigned SLA mappings and the predefined rules for the adaptation, SLA templates are updated frequently trying to reflect the actual SLAs used by service provides and consumers (step 5).

Currently, SLA mappings are defined on an XML level, where users define XSL transformations. However, a UML based GUI for the management of SLA mappings is subject of ongoing work [7].

5.2   Scenario for SLA mappings

Figure 4 depicts a scenario for defining XSL transformations. For the definition of SLA agreements we use Web Service Level Agreement (WSLA) [24]. WSLA templates are publicly available and published in a searchable registry. Each participant may download previously published WSLA templates and compare them with the local template. This can be done in an automatic way by using appropriate tools. We are currently developing a GUI that can help consumers to find suitable service categories. If there are any inconsistencies discovered, service consumer may write rules (XSL transformation) from his/her local template to the remote template. The rules can also be written by using appropriate visualization tools. Thereafter, the rules are stored in the database and can be applied during the runtime to the remote template. During the negotiation process, the transformations are performed from the remote WSLA template to the local template and vice versa.

Figure 4 depicts a service consumer generating a WSLA. The locally generated WSLA plus the rules defining transformation from local WSLA to remote WSLA, deliver a WSLA which is compliant to the remote WSLA. In the second case, the remote template has to be translated into the local one. In that case, the remote template plus the rules defining transformations from the remote to local WSLA deliver a WSLA which is compliant to the local WSLA. Thus, in this manner, the negotiation may be done using non-matching templates.

Even the service provider can define rules for XSL transformations from the publicly published WSLA templates to the local WSLA templates. Thus, both parties, provider and consumer, may match on a publicly available WSLA template.

```
  ...
  <xsl:template ...>
   <xsl:element name="Function" ...>
    <xsl:attribute name="type"> <xsl:text>Times</xsl:text> </xsl:attribute>
    <xsl:attribute name="resultType"> <xsl:text>double</xsl:text> </xsl:attribute>
    <xsl:element name="Operand" ...>
     <xsl:copy> <xsl:copy-of select="@*|node()"/> </xsl:copy>
    </xsl:element>
    <xsl:element name="Operand" ...>
    <xsl:element name="FloatScalar" ...> <xsl:text>1.27559</xsl:text> </xsl:element>
   </xsl:element>
  </xsl:element>
 </xsl:template>
  ...
```

Figure 5.   Example XSL Transformation

5.3   SLA mappings Document (SMD)

In this section, we present and discuss a sample SLA mapping document. Generally, SLA mappings can be defined using XSLT and XPath expressions.

Figure 5 shows a sample rule for XSL transformations where price defined in Euro is transformed to an equivalent price in US Dollars. Please note that for the case of simplicity we use a relatively simple example. Using XSLT even more complicated mappings can be defined, the explanation of which is out of the scope of this chapter.

As shown in Figure 5, the Euro metrics is mapped to the Dollar metric. In this example we define the mapping rule returning Dollars by using the *Times* function of *WSLA Specification* (see line 4). The *Times function* multiplies two operands: the first operand is the Dollar amount as selected in line 7, the second operand is the Dollar/Euro quote (1.27559) as specified in line 10. The dollar/euro quote can be retrieved by a Web service and is usually not hard coded.

With similar mapping rules users can map simple syntax values (values of some attributes etc.), but they can even define complex semantic mappings with considerable logic behind. Thus, even slightly different SLA templates can be translated into each other.

6.   VieSLAF framework

In this section we present the architecture used for the semi-automatic management of *meta-negotiations* and *SLA mappings*. We discuss a sample architectural case study exemplifying the usage of *Vienna Service Level Agreement Framework - VieSLAF*.

As discussed in Section 3 *VieSLAF* framework represents the first prototype for the management of self-governing ICT Infrastructures. The *VieSLAF* framework enables application developers to efficiently develop adaptable service-oriented applications simplifying the handling with numerous Web service

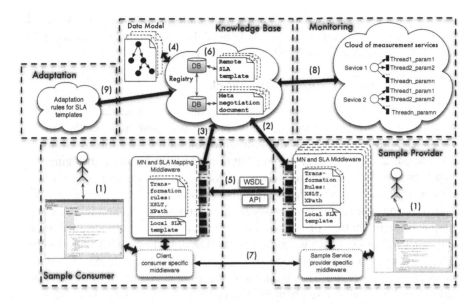

Figure 6. Extended VieSLAF Architecture with Monitoring and Taxonomies

specifications. The framework facilitates management of QoS models as for example management of meta-
negotiations [8] and SLA mappings [9]. Based on *VieSLAF* framework, a service provider may easily manage QoS models and SLA templates and frequently check whether selected services satisfy developer's needs e.g., specified QoS-parameters in SLAs. Furthermore, we discuss basic ideas about the adaptation of SLA templates.

We describe the *VieSLAF* components based on Figure 6. As shown in step (1) in Figure 6 users may access the registry using a GUI, browse through existing templates and meta-negotiation documents using the MN and SLA mapping middleware. In the next step (2), service provider specify MN documents and SLA mappings using the MN and SLA mapping middleware and submit it to the registry. Thereafter, in step (3), service consumer may query existing meta-negotiation documents, define own SLA mappings to remote templates and submit it to the registry. MN and SLA mapping middleware on both sides (provider's and consumer's) facilitates management of MNs and SLA mappings. Submitted MN documents and SLA mappings are parsed and mapped to a predefined data model (step 4). After meta-negotiation and preselection of services, service negotiation may start using the negotiation protocols, document languages, and security standards as specified in the MN document (step 5). During the negotiation SLA mappings and XSLT transformations are applied (step 6). After the negotiation, invocation of the service methods may start (step

7). SLA parameters are monitored using the monitoring service (step 8). Based on the submitted SLA mapping publicly available SLA templates are adapted reflecting the majority of local SLA templates (step 9).

7.   Conclusion and Future Work

In this chapter we have presented the goals of the Foundations of Self-Governing ICT Infrastructures (FoSII) project and how these goals can be achieved using the principles of autonomic computing. We discussed novel meta-negotiation and SLA mapping solutions for Cloud services bridging the gap between current QoS models and Cloud middleware and representing important prerequisites for the establishment of autonomic Cloud services. We discussed the approaches for meta-negotiation and SLA mapping representing partial implementation of negotiation bootstrapping and service mediation approaches. Furthermore, we presented the *VieSLAF* framework used for the management of meta-negotiations and SLA mappings. Using *VieSLAF* service users can even monitor SLA parameters during the execution of the service calls. Finally, we discussed how SLA templates can be adapted based on the submitted SLA mappings.

As the next step of the FoSII project we plan to implement bootstrapping strategies where even consumer and provider, which understand different negotiation protocols and document languages can communicate with each other.

Acknowledgments

The work described in this chapter was partially supported by the Vienna Science and Technology Fund (WWTF) under grant agreement ICT08-018 Foundations of Self-governing ICT Infrastructures (FoSII).

References

[1] R.J. Al-Ali, O.F. Rana, D.W. Walker, S. Jha, and S. Sohail. G-qosm: Grid service discovery using qos properties. Computing and Informatics, 21:363–382, 2002.

[2] Amazon Simple Storage Services (S3), http://aws.amazon.com/s3/

[3] D. Ardagna, G. Giunta, N. Ingraffia, R. Mirandola, and B. Pernici. QoS-Driven Web Services Selection in Autonomic Grid Environments. Grid Computing, High Performance and Distributed Applications (GADA) 2006 International Conference, Montpellier, France, Oct 29 - Nov 3, 2006.

[4] A. P. Barros and M. Dumas. The Rise of Web Service Ecosystems. IT Professional 8(5):31–37, Sept./Oct., 2006.

[5] J. Blythe, E. Deelman, and Y. Gil. Automatically Composed Workflows for Grid Environments. IEEE Intelligent Systems 19(4):16–23, 2004.

[6] I. Brandic, S. Pllana, and S. Benkner. Specification, Planning, and Execution of QoS-aware Grid Workflows within the Amadeus Environment. Concurrency and Computation: Practice and Experience, 20(4):331–345, John Wiley & Sons, Inc., New Jersey, March 2008.

[7] I. Brandic, D. Music, S. Dustdar, S. Venugopal, and R. Buyya. Advanced QoS Methods for Grid Workflows Based on Meta-Negotiations and SLA-Mappings. The 3rd Workshop on Workflows in Support of Large-Scale Science. In conjunction with Supercomputing 2008, Austin, TX, USA, November 17, 2008.

[8] I. Brandic, S. Venugopal, Michael Mattess, and Rajkumar Buyya, Towards a Meta-Negotiation Architecture for SLA-Aware Grid Services. Technical Report, GRIDS-TR-2008-9, Grid Computing and Distributed Systems Laboratory, The University of Melbourne, Australia, Aug. 8, 2008.

[9] I. Brandic, D. Music, P. Leitner, and S. Dustdar. VieSLAF Framework: Increasing the Versatility of Grid QoS Models by Applying Semi-automatic SLA-Mappings. Vienna University of Technology, Technical Report, TUV-184-2009-02.pdf, 2008.

[10] R. Buyya, C. S. Yeo, S. Venugopal, J. Broberg, and Ivona Brandic. Cloud Computing and Emerging IT Platforms: Vision, Hype, and Reality for Delivering Computing as the 5th Utility. Future Generation Computer Systems, ISSN: 0167-739X, Elsevier Science, Amsterdam, The Netherlands, 2009, in press, accepted on Dec. 3, 2008.

[11] K. Czajkowski, I. Foster, C. Kesselman, V. Sander and S. Tuecke. SNAP: A Protocol for Negotiating Service Level Agreements and Coordinating Resource Management in Distributed Systems. 8th Workshop on Job Scheduling Strategies for Parallel Processing, Edinburgh Scotland, July 2002.

[12] A. Dan, D. Davis, R. Kearney, A. Keller, R. King, D. Kuebler, H. Ludwig, M. Polan, M. Spreitzer, and A. Youssef. Web services on demand: WSLA-driven automated management. IBM Systems Journal, 43(1), 2004.

[13] T. Glatard, J. Montagnat, and X. Pennec. A Probabilistic Model to Analyse Workflow Performance on Production Grids. 8th IEEE International Symposium on Cluster Computing and the Grid (CCGrid 2008), Lyon, France, pages 510-517, 19-22 May 2008.

[14] Google App Engine, http://code.google.com/appengine

[15] T. Guan, E. Zaluska, and D. De Roure. A Semantic Service Matching Middleware for Mobile Devices Discovering Grid Services. Advances in Grid and Pervasive Computing, Third International Conference, GPC 2008, Kunming, China, pages 422-433, May 25-28, 2008.

[16] Foundations of Self-Governing ICT Infrastructures (FoSII) Project, http://www.wwtf.at/projects/research_projects/
details/index.php?PKEY=972_DE_O

[17] R. Jurca and B. Faltings. Reputation-based Service Level Agreements for Web Services. In Proceedings of 3rd International Conference on Service Oriented Computing, Amsterdam, The Netherlands, pages 396-409, December. 12-15, 2005.

[18] J.O. Kephart and D.M. Chess, The vision of autonomic computing. Computer, 36(1):41–50, Jan 2003.

[19] M.P. Papazoglou, P. Traverso, S. Dustdar, and F. Leymann. Service-Oriented Computing: State of the Art and Research Challenges, IEEE Computer, 40(11): 64–71, November 2007

[20] A. Paschke, J. Dietrich, and K. Kuhla. A Logic Based SLA Management Framework. Semantic Web and Policy Workshop (SWPW), 4th Semantic Web Conference (ISWC 2005), Galway, Ireland, 2005.

[21] N. Oldham, K. Verma, A. P. Sheth, and F. Hakimpour. Semantic WS-agreement partner selection. Proceedings of the 15th international conference on World Wide Web, WWW 2006, Edinburgh, Scotland, UK, May 23-26, 2006.

[22] D. Ouelhadj, J. Garibaldi, J. MacLaren, R. Sakellariou, and K. Krishnakumar. A multi-agent infrastructure and a service level agreement negotiation protocol for robust scheduling in grid computing. In Proceedings of the 2005 European Grid Computing Conference (EGC 2005), Amsterdam, The Netherlands, February, 2005.

[23] D. W. Walker, L. Huang, O. F. Rana, and Y. Huang. Dynamic service selection in workflows using performance data. Scientific Programming 15(4):235–247, 2007.

[24] Web Service Level Agreement (WSLA),
http://www.research.ibm.com/wsla/WSLASpecV1-20030128.pdf

SLA NEGOTIATION FOR VO FORMATION

Shamimabi Paurobally
School of Electronics and Computer Science
University of Westminster, London W1W 6UW, U.K
S.Paurobally@westminster.ac.uk

Abstract   Resource management systems are changing from localized resources and services towards virtual organizations (VOs) sharing millions of heterogeneous resources across multiple organizations and domains. The virtual organizations and usage models include a variety of owners and consumers with different usage, access policies, cost models, varying loads, requirements and availability. The stakeholders have private utility functions that must be satisfied and possibly maximized.

This paper proposes automated negotiation techniques between web services for the formation of virtual organizations. More specifically, a multi-issue sealed bid auction is implemented between a VO manager and potential VO members on the resources they provide or on their payment for requested resources. We evaluate our approach to show that negotiation allows to form a more efficient VO.

Keywords: Negotiation, SLA, Virtual Organisation, Agreement

P. Wieder et al. (eds.), *Grids and Service-Oriented Architectures for Service Level Agreements,*
DOI 10.1007/978-1-4419-7320-7_12, © Springer Science+Business Media, LLC 2010

1.   Introduction

Virtual Organizations (VOs) enable disparate groups of organizations and/or individuals to share resources in a controlled fashion, so that members may collaborate to achieve a shared goal [5]. Virtual organization formation occurs when a collection of grid entities, each with various problem solving capabilities and resources, agree to pool their resources together and act as a single conceptual unit seamlessly integrating their resources and services to offer the VO services. One of the challenges of Grid systems is the on demand formation of virtual organizations in open environments requiring dynamic collaborations for resource provisioning. This requires the timely orchestration and assembling of applications and services based on the resilient availability of resources in a VO. Given the dynamic nature of resources availability, predicting the resource needs and availability can be complex, and involves sensing and responding to fluctuating market trends in real time. Service providers intending to form a VO must determine the optimal set of providers to form a VO partnership with and monitor the performance of the VO during its lifetime. Existing work for managing VOs and their QoS [8][7] mainly adopt a provider-centric perspective for guaranteeing QoS for service delivery.

Given the dynamic nature of VOs and the need to incorporate service providers and consumers with diverse preferences but retaining some commonality in goals and interests, negotiation and service level agreements (SLAs) can facilitate the formation, operation and dissolution of a VO or when an outsider requests to be a new member of an existing VO. In this paper, we focus on the formation of a VO consisting of service providers through an automated negotiation between them and a VO manager. The goal is to select the set of providers that will provide the best service and resources given a set of requirements. More specifically, we implement a sealed bid auction between the VO manager and prospective VO members, and we implement three decision making strategies for the service provider and VO manager to evaluate and generate SLAs. We demonstrate the performance of such an auction compared to having no negotiation by analyzing the utility of the SLAs and the time taken to form a VO.

The remainder of the paper is structured in the following way. Section 2 presents the characteristics and requirements of VOs. Section 3 describes the sealed bid auction protocol and the process of VO formation through such an auction. Section 4 provides the strategies used by service providers on deciding how many resources to offer for joining a VO, and the strategies of a VO manager on deciding whether to accept a service provider in the VO. Section 5 analyses the performance of the sealed bid auction with respect to various strategies. Section 5 concludes.

2.   VO Characteristics

Virtual organizations are dynamic collections of individuals, institutions and resources for flexible, secure, coordinated resource sharing. The members of a VO usually consist of service providers, but a more diverse structure would also incorporate service consumers and third party servers such as for example security and authorization.

VOMS Virtual organization management (VOMs) [3], [4] services provide information on a member's state within a virtual organization in terms of his groups, roles and capabilities. DataGrid's VOMs service [4] is an account database storing VOMs credential and includes a VO manager to administrate the VO memberships. A VO Manager enrolls users and resources into the VO, allocates users to the resources and inspects the resource usage in the VO. More specifically, the VO Manager maintains a VO directory with the list of services in his VO, adds or removes groups within the VO and specifies the administrator(s) for each group within the VO. In [3], users log in to a VOM portal to get access to a restricted set of functionalities based on the role assigned to them by the VO administrator.

Membership Policies. There are several details regarding the membership policies, the foremost being enforcing access control policies to provided resources. Two different members do not necessary have the same access rights to a resource. Access rights depend on the specific resource itself, the role of the member, and possibly the recent activities of the member in the VO. VOMS also manages authorization data through a database of user roles and capabilities and a set of tools for accessing and manipulating the database, assigning roles to users and generating user credentials. A user may create an aggregate proxy certificate to access multiple VOs, which enables access to resources in any of the VOs.

Membership Expiration Time. A user membership in a VO is set for a specific duration and the authorization information and certificate are valid for a limited period of time. VO members can apply to renew their membership and certificates at the expiry time of the membership. The success of this renewal is subject to the contribution of the VO member in the VO.

Avoid over-provisioning. Investing in resources has to be leveraged with operational requirements to optimize resource utilization and costs. Membership in a VO has to consider the risk of over-provisioning and incurring excess costs.

Lifecycle of VO. A VO may be of limited duration which is either short on-demand VOs or long-lived VOs with established SLAs. A short-term VO is formed to answer a temporary need for resources and is disbanded once this need is satisfied. The policy for the formation of a VO is established dynamically.

Pathan et al. [6] propose a virtual organization model to support peering of content delivery networks (CDN). CDNs collaborate through the formation of a VO which is initiated by a CDN to meet its SLAs with its customers. Their approach is centered around the service providers and negotiation is performed through a mediator which is analogous to the VO manager in this paper. They focus more on the policy management of the VO and the mediator, abstracting away from a detailed description of auction protocol and strategies used.

Akram [2] outlines the requirements for VOs and the role of different available technologies to provide the middleware for VO formation. The paper evaluates the web services related specifications, in particular the web services resource framework, and their use in VOs. The requirements listed are informative and automated negotiation techniques can help to facilitate them for example diversity and sharing of resources between different communities.

3.   Sealed Bid Auction for VO Formation

Figure 1 shows the actors involved in a VO formation – the VO, the VO manager and the service providers outside the VO. The VO manager has a sealed bid service that will carry out a sealed bid auction with the service providers outside of the VO. The service providers advertise their resources in a directory service, and have also advertised that they provide their sealed bid service to participate in a sealed bid auction. The VO manager knows the requirements of the VO and acts on behalf of the VO to recruit new service providers according to the VO requirements. The VO manager selects suitable service providers through the directory service and conducts a sealed bid auction with them through its sealed bid service. This allows the VO manager to choose those providers which best fit the VO requirements. Thus VO formation is achieved by the VO manager adding selected service providers as members of the VO.

3.1   Sealed Bid Auction Service

Figure 2 illustrates the sealed bid auction protocol implementing the VO formation. Let SP denote the set of service providers that the VO manager m selects from the directory service. The auction is started by the VO manager's sealed bid service issuing a broadcast to all providers in SP. The content of the broadcast is a measure of the resources that the VO manager expects to be provided, for example 10 GB per hour. A service provider's sealed bid service in SP checks the provider's available resources and decides if it can make a bid to satisfy m's broadcast. If the service provider can make a bid, then the provider's sealed bid service generates its bid and send this privately to m. This is different from English auctions such as eBay since bidders are not privy to each other's bids. The VO manager m receives all bids privately, evaluates them and chooses which bids to accept. Here m may choose to accept more than one

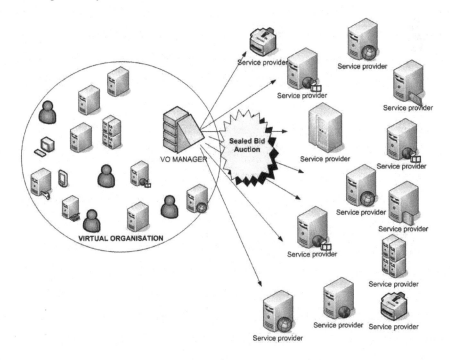

Figure 1. Actors in Virtual Organisation Formation

bid and to reject the rest. We explain our decision making algorithms in section 4.

For the VO manager and the providers to perform a sealed bid auction, they expose their sealed bid service. Figure 2 shows a sealed bid auction. A VO manager's sealed bid service exposes the method private_bid for service providers to invoke this method and submit their bids. In the case of a service provider's auction service, its exposed methods are broadcast for the VO manager to invoke as a call for bids, accept and reject for the VO manager to respectively accept or reject the provider's bid.

Figures 3 and 4 respectively give an overview of the port-type of the sealed bid auction service for the VO manager and a service provider. In addition the VO manager exposes the do_auction to initialize the VO manager's sealed bid auction service.

3.2   Service Level Agreement (SLA)

The nature of agreements is dependent on the type of resource being provided. An SLA is a list of agreement terms and we define a structure called Service_Level_Agreement in WSDL to describe the resources being negoti-

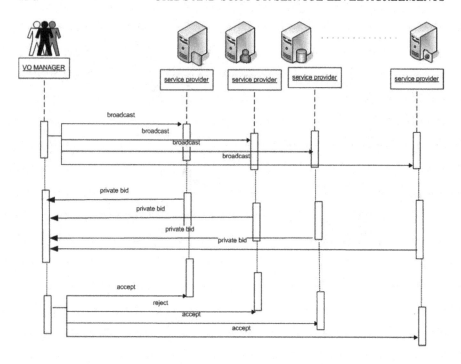

Figure 2.   Sealed Bid Auction between VO Manager and Service Providers

```
<!-- SEALED BID AUCTION PORT-TYPE FOR THE VO MANAGER -->
<wsdl:portType name="Sealed_Bid_Manager">
  <wsdl:operation name="do_auction"
    parameterOrder="Context_Job provider_list">
  </wsdl:operation>

  <wsdl:operation name="private_bid" parameterOrder="Bid">
    <wsdl:input message="impl:BidIn" name="BidIn"/>
    <wsdl:output message="impl:BidOut" name="BidOut"/>
  </wsdl:operation>
</wsdl:portType>
```

Figure 3.   Sealed Bid Auction PortType for the VO manager

ated upon. The parameters of a broadcast, private_bid, accept and reject method invocations are passed as Service_Level_Agreement types.

A Service_Level_Agreement is essentially a list of issues characterizing the resource or task in terms of an SLA. The SLA structure is simpler that a WS-Agreement structure [1]. Each term in an SLA includes a name, a value and a flag indicating whether it is a qualitative or a quantitative term. For example, a service description term may include (Provider_SHA, Auction_227,

```
<!-- SEALED BID AUCTION PORT-TYPE FOR A SERVICE PROVIDER -->
<wsdl:portType name="Sealed_Bid_Provider">
   <wsdl:operation name="broadcast" parameterOrder="call_for_bids">
    <wsdl:input message="impl:call_for_bidsIn" name="call_for_bidsIn"/>
    <wsdl:output message="impl:call_for_bidsOut" name="call_for_bidsOut"/>
   </wsdl:operation>

   <wsdl:operation name="accept" parameterOrder="SLA">
    <wsdl:input message="impl:SLAIn" name="SLAIn"/>
    <wsdl:output message="impl:SLAOut" name="SLAOut"/>
   </wsdl:operation>

   <wsdl:operation name="reject" parameterOrder="Rejection">
    <wsdl:input message="impl:RejectionIn" name="RejectionIn"/>
    <wsdl:output message="impl:RejectionOut" name="RejectionOut"/>
   </wsdl:operation>
</wsdl:portType>
```

Figure 4.   Sealed Bid Auction PortType for a service provider

```
{(price,50, IsQuantitative),
(StorageCapacity, 1GB, IsQuantitative),
(location, London, NonQuantitative)} ).
```
In such a bid, the SLA terms are price, StorageCapacity and location, and the associated values indicate that particular bid.

4. Decision Making Strategies

In this section, we describe our decision making algorithms for the evaluation and the generation of the SLA and SLA templates. The VO manager generates an SLA template for the broadcast invocation and evaluates the SLA offers sent by service providers in their private bids to choose which bid to accept. A service provider evaluates the broadcast from the VO manager and generates an SLA to send as a private bid. An accepted bid by the VO manager is considered as an SLA between the VO manager and that bidding service provider. In all of these cases, the functions are calculated according to the requirements and preferences of the VO manager and the service provider as applicable. Thus, in making a bid, a service provider considers its available resources and how long it should reserve these resources for the VO.

4.1 A Provider's SLA Evaluation and Generation

A service provider has three decision making strategies – 1) cost and profit strategy, 2) truth-telling strategy and 3) decrement strategy. In the truth-telling strategy, a service provider reveals its requirements and preferences. The VO manager may also have a truth-telling strategy when sending a broadcast SLA with its preferred value for each agreement terms. A service provider's bid is grounded with the provider's own preferred value for each issue. If the broadcast SLA lies outside the reserve values (maximum and minimum values for an issue or term) for the service provider, then the latter's bid is instantiated with its reserve values.

In the cost and profit strategy, on receiving a broadcast, a service provider evaluates whether it is worthwhile to submit a bid according to the profits it may achieve. The cost and profit strategy is dependent on the resources available for that service provider in the system for each service i. Assume at time t, a provider p has resources α_i^t already reserved, and that it has a total resources *capability* of r_{total}. The auction starts with the broadcast SLA $\alpha(\text{VO\_R})$ from the VO manager. Let $\kappa_i^t(\alpha)$ denote the resources that service provider p has to commit to the new VO at time t and VO_R denote the resource specification. The *added cost* of providing resources $\kappa_i^t(\alpha)$ at time t for provider p is denoted by $AC_i(\alpha(\text{VO\_R}) \mid \alpha_i^t)$:

$$AC_i(\alpha(\text{VO\_R}) \mid \alpha_i^t) = r_{total}(\alpha(\text{VO\_R}) \cup \alpha_i^t) - r_{total}(\alpha_i^t)$$

The added effort for provider p of making a bid and providing resources is the difference between 1) its current resource allocation added to provisioning a new VO according to the broadcast SLA and 2) the cost of only its current resource allocation. If $AC_i(\alpha(\text{VO\_R}) \mid \alpha_i^t) < threshold\_profit(\text{VO\_R})$, then the provider can make a bid; otherwise, it will not bid. $threshold\_profit(\text{VO\_R})$ is the provider's perceived reward for provisioning the new VO. A service provider looking for a reward will bid if equation 1 is satisfied, where current_profit is the profit it currently achieves from its current resource allocation.

$$AC_i(\alpha(\text{VO\_R})) < (threshold\_profit(\text{VO\_R}) + current\_profit) \quad (1)$$

In the Decrement strategy, the service provider and the VO manager have an evaluation and generation margin. The service provider evaluates a broadcast SLA and generates a bid against these pre-defined margins above or below the reserve values, depending if it prefers a low or high value for that resource. This is to give the stakeholders a chance to converge, independent of the time left, to an agreement instead of rejecting the broadcast SLA rightaway.

4.2   A VO Manager's Evaluation of a Bid

The VO manager chooses the bids that it will accept by considering both the requirements of the VO and computing those bids with the highest utility that falls within the VO manager's requirements. For example, there are only four new memberships available for that VO. Thus if there are 10 bids, then the VO manager chooses the four best bids out of these ten bids, which may depend on the other agreement terms in addition to the extra storage offered. The evaluation function for choosing the best bids depends on the utility for the manager of each term in the received bids along with their offered values. More specifically, equation 2 defines the overall utility of a bid for the VO manager m as U_{bid}^m – this is the normalized weighted summation of the utility of the individual agreement terms V_j^i for that bid.

$$U_{bid}^m = \sum_{1 \le j \le n} \omega_j^i V_j^i(bid[j]) \tag{2}$$

5. Evaluation of the Auction for VO Formation

We deployed the sealed bid service over Globus Toolkit and evaluated the sealed bid service for VO formation. The terms of the SLA regarding the resources offered by a service provider include the identifier of the provider, the auction identifier, the size of the submitted job, the processing rate and the response time. We measure the utility gained by a provider to form part of a VO through the sealed bid auction against time taken to reach the agreement.

From the VO's perspective we measure the time taken to recruit five members in the VO with respect to the utility of the agreed SLA. We vary the strategies to compare between them. We compare the performance of the sealed bid service with the case of no negotiations. No negotiations mean that the VO manager broadcasts the SLA and the service provider either replies that it accepts to provision the broadcast or not. Thus no negotiation implies no bids from the service providers.

Figure 5. Utility gained for Provider against time to reach SLA

Figure 6. Time to form VO against Member numbers

Figure 7.   Utility gained for Manager against time to reach SLA

Figure 5 shows the average utility obtained by the providers for the exchanged SLAs against time. The service provider obtains the least utility when there is no negotiation because it has to accept the VO manager's broadcast SLA if the provider wants to be part of the VO. The truth telling strategy performs better for the service provider at first because it obtains a better SLA from the VO manager than when the latter is using a Decrement strategy. However a better final SLA is obtained using the decrement strategy because the bid made by the service provider is better than when using the truth telling strategy. Finally the cost endowment strategy performs the best for the service provider because it takes into account the available resources of the provider.

Figure 6 shows the time to agree on an SLA and form a VO from the service provider's perspective. The time for VO formation is plotted with respect to the number of members joining in the VO. In this case, not having any negotiation saves the most time and if any agreement is possible from the broadcast message, then the SLA is reached straightaway. However without negotiation, less providers agree to join the VO, and more providers reject the manager's broadcast. Moreover, the more complex the decision strategy, the more time is taken to agree on an SLA and form a VO. However, the truth telling strategy being the least complex strategy with negotiation takes less time, but only a few providers agree to join the VO. Thus, using the cost and profit strategy, all the service providers manage to reach an agreement and form an SLA, leading to a VO with the most members with this strategy.

Figure 7 shows the average utility obtained by the VO manager for the exchanged SLAs against time. Since the "no negotiation" case is designed in favor of the VO manager where a service provider can only accept or reject the VO manager's broadcast SLA, the VO manager achieves high utility in the early stages when there is no negotiation. However, the manager would achieve a low utility if it had to accept a service provider's broadcast message if the protocol was reversed. As time elapses, the decrement and cost and profit strategies performs better than no negotiation because there are more service providers joining in the VO when there is a sealed bid auction. Furthermore, the VO manager can compare and choose the best providers as opposed when not negotiating. In the end, the truth-telling strategy achieves the same utility as when no negotiation. Thus the VO manager is not worse off by carrying out a sealed bid auction, and in the long run achieves more utility with negotiation.

6. Conclusions

On demand resilient VO formation and operation in a dynamic, open and competitive environment is a key challenge of Grid systems. Many areas have started working on Grid computing business applications, for example, financial services for running complex financial models and online games with highly parallel multi-player online games. In this paper, we propose a negotiation protocol, namely a sealed bid auction protocol for the dynamic formation of virtual organizations between a VO manager and prospective service providers. We implemented three decision strategies and evaluation of our auctioning protocol shows the benefit of negotiation over not having any negotiation. Through negotiation, the utility of the obtained SLAs is higher and the number of service providers accepting to join the VO increases. Furthermore, the VO manager can choose the most suitable providers by comparing bids. Future work involves investigating the operation and dynamic re-formation of VOs, and the heterogeneous negotiation between both service providers and consumers to join a VO.

References

[1] A. Andrieux, K. Czajkowski, A. Dan, K. Keahey, H. Ludwig, J. Pruyne, J. Rofrano, S. Tuecke, and M. Xu. March 2007. Web Services Agreement Specification (WS-Agreement). http://forge.gridforum.org/sf/projects/graap-wg.

[2] A. Akram. WSRF based virtual Organisation Middleware. In Proceedings of 18th Annual IRMA International Conference, Vancouver, British Columbia, Canada, May 2007.

[3] S. Asif, K. Marko, S. Newhouse, and J. Darlington. ICENI Virtual Organisation Management. In UK e-Science All Hands Meeting, Nottingham, UK, September 2003, pages 117–120, September 2003.

[4] DataGrid. Virtual organization membership service. http://edg-wp2.web.cern.ch/edg-wp2/security/voms/voms.html.

[5] I. Foster, C. Kesselman, and S. Tuecke. The anatomy of the grid: Enabling scalable virtual organisations. International Journal of Supercomputer Applications, 15(3):200–222, 2001.

[6] A. Pathan, J. Broberg, K. Bubendorfer, K. Kim, and R. Buyya. An Architecture for Virtual Organisation (VO)-Based Effective Peering of Content Delivery Networks. In Proceedings of UPGRADE-CN 2007, June 2007.

[7] G. Shercliff, P. Stockreisser, J. Shao, W. Gray, and N. Fiddian. Supporting QoS Assessment and Monitoring in Virtual Organisations. In Proceedings of IEEE International Conference on Services Computing. IEEE Computer Society, 2005.

[8] Jun Wen and Xianliang Lu. The design of QOS guarantee network subsystem. SIGOPS Operating Systems Review, 36(1):81–87, 2002.

FROM SERVICE MARKETS TO SERVICE ECONOMIES – AN INFRASTRUCTURE FOR PROTOCOL-GENERIC SLA NEGOTIATIONS

Sebastian Hudert

Department of Information Systems Management,
University of Bayreuth, Universitaetsstr. 30, 95447 Bayreuth,
Germany
sebastian.hudert@uni-bayreuth.de

Abstract   Visions of 21st century's information systems show highly specialized digital services and resources, interacting continuously and with a global reach. For a broad adoption of this vision in a commercial context it is crucial to have a mechanism in place to guarantee quality of service and to decentrally coordinate the involved resources. Current service infrastructures try to tackle these problems by applying socioeconomic mechanisms such as electronic negotiations and service level agreements. Such technologies allow for the implementation of electronic service markets in analogy to real-world markets for everyday goods. However, economic theory claims that different market situations and negotiated products (i.e. SLAs) demand different negotiation protocols in order to reach the highest-possible overall efficiency of the system. Thus we argue that next generation service infrastructures will be based on a global service economy where several different service markets and thus protocols are present at any given point in time. In this paper we present a novel approach for such an infrastructure, based on structured protocol descriptions and software-agent technology.

Keywords: service level agreement negotiation, quality of service, service economy, negotiation protocol, software agents,

P. Wieder et al. (eds.), *Grids and Service-Oriented Architectures for Service Level Agreements,*
DOI 10.1007/978-1-4419-7320-7_13, © Springer Science+Business Media, LLC 2010

1.   Introduction

Visions of 21st century's information systems show highly specialized digital services and resources, which interact continuously and with a global reach. Today's Internet of mainly human interaction evolves towards a socio-technical and global information infrastructure, where humans as well as software agents acting on their behalf continuously interact to exchange data and computational resources. Such infrastructures will possibly consist of millions of service providers (SP), consumers (SC) and a multitude of possible intermediaries like brokers, workflow orchestrators and others, thus forming an economic environment. Electronic services and resources traded on a global scope will eventually realize the vision of an open and global service economy, sometimes also called the Internet of Services (IoS) [15].

For a broad adoption of this vision in a commercial context it is important to have a mechanism in place to guarantee quality of service (QoS) for each service invocation, even across enterprise boundaries. This becomes crucial when parts of mission critical workflows will be executed on external services. A very simple use case would be an engineering company purchasing basic storage and computation services from the Amazon Web Services (AWS) [1] as well as specific fluid simulation services from a specialized application SP. Since such scenarios inherently lack the applicability of centralized QoS management, guarantees must be obtained in the form of bi- or even multi-lateral service level agreements (SLAs) assuring service quality across individual sites [12]. SCs can thus benefit from SLAs because they make nonfunctional properties of services predictable and subsequently the corresponding services dependable as needed in a business context. In order to support a comprehensive SLA-based management for such settings, the main phases of the SLA life cycle should be directly supported by the underlying infrastructure: service discovery, negotiation, SLA creation, service binding, execution and post processing (such as rating the service or payment). Following the rationale of economic theory we propose an infrastructure for supporting the discovery and flexible, thus protocol-generic, negotiation of SLAs as a first step towards distributed systems incorporating the above mentioned ideas.

In doing so we will first derive a detailed scenario model for the envisioned architectures of next generation computing systems in section 2. Building on this model we define the research goal underlying this work and conduct a comprehensive requirements analysis for the infrastructure to be designed (3). In section 4 we give an overview on related research projects and show how current efforts still fail to fulfill at least some of the identified requirements. Subsequently we present the design of our own infrastructure aiming at closing

---

[1] http://aws.amazon.com

this gap between conceptual requirements and currently available technology in section 5. We will conclude this paper with a short conclusion and overview on future work.

2.   Vision for Next Generation Distributed Computing: Service Economies

In order to derive a model for future service systems it is crucial to understand the paradigms that are currently employed in distributed information systems and identify similarities and differences. Based on these developments a trend of ideas and paradigms can be extracted leading to a well-founded scenario definition for our work.

The technical paradigm underlying most of the developments in distributed information systems in the recent years is the service orientation (SO). The main idea of SO is that every function offered by humans, organizational entities or computer systems, is viewed as an abstract service, which in turn can again be combined with other services to create more complex composite services and so forth. According to the general agreement in the literature a service as applied in SO systems thus represents an individually addressable software component that [7]

- provides some functionality to a service requester,

- can be accessed over an electronic network, such as the Internet,

- hides technical implementation details from the SC, as it only advertises its interface

- and is loosely coupled to the other services and SCs. (This means that their interactions are not hardcoded in each individual service, but every SC discovers and binds a given other service it interacts with at runtime. This is already exploited in electronic service markets today, where formerly unknown SP and SC components even automatically negotiate over a prospective service invocation; see for example CATNETS[2] or SORMA[3]).

Additionally another paradigm for distributed coordination of electronic resources, crossing organizational boundaries emerged: Grid Computing (GC). GC is mainly concerned with "coordinated resource sharing and problem solving in dynamic, multi-institutional virtual organizations" [8]thus first and foremost representing systems that "coordinate [...] resources that are not subject

---

[2]http://www.catnets.uni-bayreuth.de
[3]http://www.sorma-project.org

to centralized control" [6], ranging from computational and storage resources to code repositories [8]. In doing so GC systems attempt "to deliver nontrivial qualities of service", following the vision of the "utility of the combined system [being] significantly greater than that of the sum of its parts" [6].

Building on GC and SO technologies and virtualization techniques, the most recent trend in distributed computing was realized: Cloud Computing (CC). Buyya defines CC as: "[...] a type of parallel and distributed system consisting of a collection of interconnected and virtualized computers [...] presented as one or more unified computing resources based on service level agreements established through negotiation between the service provider and consumers" [4]. Following this rationale Liu and Orban also stress the fact that these services are remotely consumed on demand [10].

All of these developments in today's distributed systems point to the same vision of the future Internet based on highly dynamic networks of composable services, offered and consumed on demand and on a global scope.

On a technical side it can be observed that all current paradigms build on very similar interaction technologies. The majority of services employ Web Service standards and the Internet as a communication platform. On the other hand these infrastructures differ slightly in the way the individual services are managed and used on a higher abstraction level. This is especially noticeable when looking for example at the applied invocation paradigms. However, not building on different technologies but only using them differently should not prevent a development of consolidation and integration of paradigms as a next step towards more powerful and efficient global systems. This is what many experts in research and industry envision as the next step in distributed computing and business, an economy of electronic services.

This vision takes the main idea of SO, the design of distributed systems in terms of interoperable and composable services, one step further. It rigorously focuses on the goal of an Internet-based service economy similar to the real-world service sector. Digital services will be offered over digital service markets, purchased by respective customers and then combined with internal or other external services to business workflows of varying complexity. Such a service economy will explicitly focus on the orchestration of a number of services from outside and inside a company to achieve higher utilities than the individual services would, just as GC. As proposed with the CC paradigm services will be invoked on demand and therefore have to be deployed on virtualized platforms to satisfy the QoS restrictions posed by the customers. In addition to the combination of these concepts the envisioned settings will focus much more on new business models and the commercial application of the SO ideas. These will concern trading processes down to the level of an individual service, and the subsequent charging based solely on its usage and delivered QoS. In such a system even very small and specialized companies can find a niche in the digital economy where they can compete with the ubiquitous international companies, which in turn have to face a much higher competition on a global market, ultimately leading to increasing service quality [5].

Summarizing the service economy scenario model results in the following set of characteristics [15]:

- The IoS focuses on a (potentially huge) set of electronic services of varying complexity.

- These services will be employed in potentially mission-critical business processes and thus have to fulfill a (pre-negotiated) set of QoS guarantees as stated in a SLA.

- New business models will cope with the possibility of trading even individual services and charging them based on their actual usage.

- It will consist of a global set of SPs, SCs negotiating over digital services employing some mediating nodes such as service brokers and market makers.

Arguably, other scenarios for the future Internet are also possible, for example ones in which only very basic services, and thus SLAs, are traded, just as with current CC platforms. However, a scenario more or less similar to our model seems the most probable, given the current and past developments.

3. Research Goal and Requirements

Two of the main challenges for future SEs from a commercial perspective are reliability of the services traded and the technical infrastructure underlying the service economy. In such settings the need for guaranteed reliability and service quality becomes more prominent, as no longer the question of who provides the service matters but only whether he is able to achieve the requested result. Negotiated service quality guarantees are to be stated in potentially very fine-grained SLAs between SC and SP, acting as a signed contract governing the subsequent service invocation [4]. Based on such a SLA the actual execution of the service can be monitored in order to assess the compliance to the contract, eventually triggering some corrective measures in case of a SLA violation.

Additionally, differences in system configuration, or the services actually traded, demand different negotiation protocols in order to reach the highest-possible efficiency of the overall system. Each of the individual domains depicted above potentially favors a different negotiation protocol (e.g. Grids that favor Reverse Auctions for job submitters to buy standardized Grid Services from multiple providers, whereas SO systems, due to the potentially very complex services, will probably favor bargaining protocols). Based on these findings and the global context of the envisioned scenario it is not likely or even efficient, that only one central marketplace for electronic services will emerge, offering a single, known protocol. Instead a system of marketplaces offering different protocols probably will emerge, each of which will best be suited for a given set of negotiated services in a specific context.

Fortifying this, we argue that restricting SCs or SPs in that they are only able to interact with one distinct service market, e.g. the domain they were implemented for (GC or CC), and are therefore only technically compatible with the applied negotiation protocol for this domain, unnecessarily decreases the potential flexibility and efficiency of the whole system. SC should be able to buy, and therefore negotiate about, any fitting service, regardless of the market it is offered in and thus regardless of the protocol with which they are offered. Additionally, given the dynamic nature of distributed workflow executions and the increased complexity of global service selection manual negotiations of the human users are by far not efficient enough. This process should be automated by electronic software agents that negotiate on the users' behalf.

Research Goal.   The research goal of this work is thus to develop a generic, service-based architecture as well as a set of protocols and data structures acting as a basic infrastructure for software agents to discover and negotiate about electronic services independent of the actual negotiation protocols applied.

Requirements Analysis.   We will now derive a set of conceptual requirements for a service management overlay that aims at supporting the flexible discovery and negotiation of services for SLA-based service economies.

Requirements for the discovery phase:

- After the discovery phase all parties must have a common understanding of the protocol to be executed in the negotiation phase [11].

- This common understanding must be generated dynamically at runtime [3].

Requirements for the negotiation phase - Negotiation Object:

- Services (and thus SLAs) of different complexity must be negotiable [13].

- Possible offers should be restrictable, incl. non-negotiable SLA terms [17]. This allows for the distinction of service properties that are under negotiation and those that aren't.

Negotiation phase - Protocol / Setting:

- Different marketplaces and protocols (fixed-price catalogues, bargaining, auctions etc.) even within one market are needed for different services to be traded [13].

- Service requesters and consumers must be able to start the negotiation [17]. This way not only a request for a service can be communicated but also a service offering can be actively proposed to potential SCs.

Negotiation phase - Strategy / Participants:

- Software agents should act as negotiators [11].

- Negotiators must be able to act on different markets, even simultaneously [3].

- Intermediaries, such as auctioneers or brokers, should be present.

Before presenting the architectural design of our work we will now give an overview on related research efforts in that area.

4.   Related Work

The commercial vision of a service economy heavily builds on negotiation theory and different negotiation protocols developed therein. Such negotiation protocols crucially define a negotiation's outcome by "determin[ing] the way offers and messages [...] are exchanged" [2, p. 317]. As a next step these findings are ported to the digital world, forming the new research discipline of Electronic Negotiations [2]. On the one hand respective researchers came up with formal descriptions and characterizations of given negotiation protocols, on the other hand increasing computing power allowed for the definition of new negotiation protocols, which would not work efficiently with human negotiators, such as multi-attribute auctions.

Additionally scientists constantly improved software agent technologies, finally allowing for the implementation of very complex bidding strategies in a fully automated fashion [14]. International research projects such as SORMA bring the vision of agent-based service markets to life in Grid environments. ZIMORY[4] can be seen as an industrial implementation of a service market, though not based on software agents.

QoS guarantees (as well as SLAs as their contractual representation) have risen after traditional distributed systems came to maturity and reliability came into focus. Significant work was done in the area of SLA languages or architectures of SLA based systems by researchers such as Ludwig and Keller [12]or Yarmolenko and Sakellariou [16]. An ever growing amount of research projects, such as CoreGRID[5] already employ SLAs for resource management and thus have done the first step towards our infrastructure vision. However, they still lack a integration of multiple negotiation protocols and service markets

---

[4]http://www.zimory.com
[5]http://www.coregrid.net

at runtime. Nevertheless the ongoing Web Services Agreement [1]standardization effort at the Open Grid Forum[6] shows the growing interest for SLA-based infrastructures from both research and industry.

Surprisingly, there is little research done in combining the economic considerations concerning negotiations on the one hand and QoS/SLA developments on the other hand. As the GC projects pioneered in combining digital resources on a large scale, mostly Grid projects stand out in terms of developed SLA negotiation mechanisms. However even those projects mainly focus on static and centralized architectures within which only one particular, and fixed, negotiation protocol is implemented, e.g. OntoGrid [14]using the (Iterated) ContractNet or NextGRID[7] the Discrete Offers Protocol). Hence those systems allow for the definition of individual service markets. However such systems such systems still lack the possibility for SCs and even SPs to migrate at runtime from one market to another (in analogy to a real-world economy).

Although a common understanding states the need for flexible negotiations, only a few research efforts incorporate the mere possibility of different protocols in SLA negotiations. [11] and [3]being two of the most prominent examples. However, those frameworks still lack important flexibility by restricting the negotiation protocols to a small and fixed set and by building on static, centralized architectures without appropriate discovery mechanisms.

5.   Design Proposal for a protocol-generic SLA Discovery and Negotiation Infrastructure

The traditional service usage cycle is no longer suitable in the envisioned settings. It has to be extended by the means to integrate SLA negotiations in a flexible way. Figure 1 presents such an extended service usage cycle suitable for the envisioned SEs.

When discovering a required service, the agents thus have to perform an additional step within the discovery phase compared to the traditional cycle: they have to discover the negotiation protocol description document(s) associated with this given service, too. This way, the basis for the decision among competing services is broadened by the knowledge in which way a SP offers an acceptable SLA negotiation style.

Subsequently the agents negotiate about the service, according to the protocol as described in the description document, and create the SLA. From here on the process adheres to the traditional service usage cycle and executes the binding, execution and release steps. However, in a commercial setting additional

---

[6]http://www.ogf.org
[7]http://www.nextgrid.org/

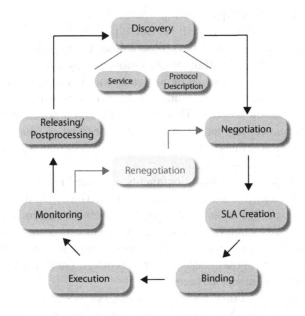

Figure 1. Service Usage Cycle in an electronic Service Economy

monitoring may become crucial as well as optional post-processing steps, such as the rating of a given transaction partner.

The abstract design idea of our infrastructure, building on the above mentioned requirements, is to define a digital negotiation protocol description in such a way, that software agents can both parse and subsequently interpret it in a fully automated fashion.

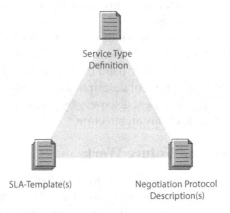

Figure 2. Triangular Relationship between Service Description Documents

A triangular relationship as seen in figure 2 between the involved, service-related documents will be created: service type definition (e.g. its interface), SLA (template) and the respective protocol description(s). Service interfaces represent the core concept within the SO vision, as they define the service's capabilities independent of its actual implementation. SLA templates are basically not completely filled in and agreed upon SLAs, which are to be finalized during the actual negotiation process. This way the SP can a priori specify ranges of possible guarantees and thus limit the actual negotiation space. Finally the protocol description defines how an SLA (probably based on a given template) for a given service can be negotiated.

Building on these description documents, a layered reference architecture for a service economy as we envision it can be derived. On the lowest layer the actual services (SP) are located along with their consumers (SC). Each of those is directly associated with a service management agent on the Service Management Layer, in analogy to [1]. These agents are responsible for the efficient management of the underlying services in terms of selling or purchasing other services from the service layer.

As opposed to traditional views on service systems our approach further subclassifies the Service Management Layer into a Market Layer and an Economy Layer. The former comprises all management agents acting as market participants and negotiating over service invocations (thus over SLAs) as well as a set of optionally used market intermediaries such as brokers or market makers. Many of today's research projects aim at this layer and, what is even more important, implement SC and SP components for only this layer, moreover for one particular market present in this layer (characterized among others by a distinct negotiation protocol). In our view another layer must be introduced enabling SPs and most importantly SCs to migrate between individual service markets and adapt to the new context. In supporting this task a distributed infrastructure of service document registries is needed similar to those currently present in individual service markets.

From a data perspective the individual SPs and SCs have a set of private data concerning reservation values for the SLA negotiations, utility functions or offered starting prices. On the other hand the service description documents, such as SLA templates and protocol descriptions, are openly published at the registry infrastructure for subsequent discovery by potential transaction partners. Figure 4 gives an overview of this architecture.

6.   Conclusion and Future Work

In this paper we argued for a development in distributed computing from service markets, as present today, towards service economies as a paradigm for future distributed computing environments. In doing so we derived a de-

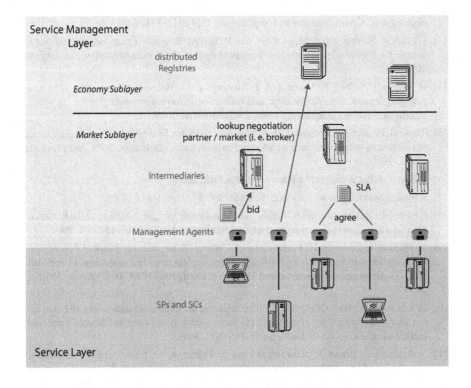

Figure 3.   Abstract Architecture of the future Service Economy

tailed scenario model for this vision and deducted a set of requirements for infrastructures supporting it. Building on these requirements we presented a novel architecture design based on a set of structured description documents and employing software agent technology.

Current and future work comprises the definition of a protocol description language ([9]) as well as the implementation of a proof-of-concept prototype for our approach. Once this system is finished, we will conduct extensive evaluation runs to investigate how such a system of many different services and protocols performs compared to single-protocol markets regarding efficiency and robustness.

References

[1] A. Andrieux, K. Czajkowski, A. Dan, K. Keahey, H. Ludwig, T. Nakata, J. Pruyne, J. Rofrano, S. Tuecke, and M. Xu. Web services agreement specification, version 03/2007. 2007.

[2] M. Bichler, G. Kersten, and S. Strecker. Towards a structured design of electronic negotiations. Group Decision and Negotiation, 12(4):311–335, 2003.

[3] I. Brandic, S. Venugopal, M. Mattess, and R. Buyya. Towards a meta-negotiation architecture for sla-aware grid services. Technical Report, University of Melbourne, August 2008.

[4] R. Buyya, C.S. Yeo, S. Venugopal, J. Broberg, and I. Brandic. Cloud computing and emerging it platforms: Vision, hype, and reality for delivering computing as the 5th utility. Future Generation Computer Systems, 25(6):599–616, 2009.

[5] Theseus Project Consortium. Texo business webs im Internet der Dienste (german). http://theseus-programm.de/anwendungsszenarien/texo/default.aspx, 2009. last checked: 13. 01. 2010.

[6] I. Foster. What is the grid? a three point checklist, 2002.

[7] I. Foster. Service-oriented science. Science, 308(5723):814–817, 2005.

[8] I. Foster, C. Kesselman, and S. Tuecke. The anatomy of the grid: Enabling scalable virtual organizations. International Journal of Supercomputer Applications, 15:2001, 2001.

[9] S. Hudert, T. Eymann, H. Ludwig, and G. Wirtz. A negotiation protocol description language for automated service level agreement negotiations. In Proceedings of the 11th IEEE Conference on Commerce and Enterprise Computing (CEC 09), Vienna, Austria, 2009.

[10] H. Liu and D. Orban. Gridbatch: Cloud computing for large-scale data-intensive batch applications. In Proceedings of the 8th IEEE International Symposium on Cluster Computing and the Grid 2008 (CCGRID08), pages 295–305, 2008.

[11] A. Ludwig, P. Braun, R. Kowalczyk, and B. Franczyk. A framework for automated negotiation of service level agreements in services grids. In Lecture Notes in Computer Science, Proceedings of the Workshop on Web Service Choreography and Orchestration for Business Process Management, 2006, Vol. 3812/2006, 2006.

[12] H. Ludwig, A. Keller, A. Dan, R. King, and R. Franck. A service level agreement language for dynamic electronic services. Journal of Electronic Commerce Research, 3:43–59, 2003.

[13] D. Neumann, J. Stoesser, C. Weinhardt, and J. Nimis. A framework for commercial grids - economic and technical challenges. Journal of Grid Computing, 6(3):325–347, September 2008. ISSN: 1570-7873.

[14] S. Paurobally, V. Tamma, and M. Wooldridge. A framework for web service negotiation. ACM Trans. Auton. Adapt. Syst., 2(4):14, 2007.

[15] C. Schroth and T. Janner. Web 2.0 and SOA: Converging concepts enabling the internet of services. IT Professional, 9(3):36–41, 2007.

[16] V. Yarmolenko and R. Sakellariou. Towards increased expressiveness in service level agreements: Research articles. Concurr. Comput. : Pract. Exper., 19(14):1975–1990, 2007.

[17] W. Ziegler, O. Waeldrich, Ph. Wieder, T. Nakata, and M. Parkin. Considerations for negotiation and monitoring of service level agreements. Technical Report TR-0167, CoreGRID, June 2008.

SERVICE LEVEL AGREEMENTS IN BREIN

Bastian Koller
Hoechstleistungsrechenzentrum Stuttgart, Stuttgart, Germany
koller@hlrs.de

Henar Munoz Frutos
Telefonica Investigacin y Desarrollo S.A, Spain
henar@tid.es

Giuseppe Laria
Centro di Ricerca in Matematica Pura ed Applicata, University of Salerno, Italy
laria@crmpa.unisa.it

Abstract   With electronic business (eBusiness) becoming ubiquitous, the traditional ways of doing commerce need to be changed or completely replaced to support the end users effectively in performing their business. This includes especially the representation of business relationships with an electronic format to allow for automated processing of the respective parts of e.g. contractual obligations. One prominent representation tool are Service Level Agreements. Conceptually established as paper representation to describe parts of contracts of telecom operators, SLAs have become a research topic in the ICT domain now since several years.

However, the current State of the Art in Service Level Agreements and their management, still shows several deficits, which prevented the uptake of eBusiness solutions (based on Service Level Agreements) so far. This paper will present how the BREIN project enhanced, amongst others Service Level Agreement Management with capabilities from the Multiagent and Semantic domain, to provide an enhanced solution, compared to existing technologies. Thereby the main emphasize was on basing the developments on existing results to concentrate on gap filling instead of re-invention of the wheel.

Keywords: BREIN, SLA Management, SLA lifecycle, Semantic Annotations, Multiagent Negotiation, SA-SLA, SLA Schema, WS-Agreement, WSLA

P. Wieder et al. (eds.), *Grids and Service-Oriented Architectures for Service Level Agreements*,
DOI 10.1007/978-1-4419-7320-7_14, © Springer Science+Business Media, LLC 2010

1.   Introduction

Todays market needs get more and more complex every day. As opposed to the past where Service Providers could establish their business in a known and limited domain, today a flexible adaptation of their service portfolio is needed. Especially to ensure competitiveness with other players.

Whilst this adaptation is a 'non-blocker' for huge market players (once they decide to adapt a service and its capabilities, they can invest in this), this has a huge impact on Small and Medium Enterprises (SMEs). As they are often bound to their specialized services, enhancements/adaptations would imply high investments, which is simply not affordable for them.

With regard to this, the concept of outsourcing is still seen as an key enabler for increasing the competitiveness of SME. Especially in the electronic business (eBusiness) market, this implies to ensure that outsourcing and collaborations are supported in a proper way, to guarantee the correct execution of services with respect to guaranteed (and agreed upon) obligations. All this, by not putting more burden on the respective end users but rather simplifying the access to and use of eBusiness platforms in an intelligent way.

The BREIN [1] project was created to exactly address this support by enhancing the classical Grid solutions by integrating Multiagent and Semantic Web concepts to a dynamic, standard based environment for eBusiness. Thereby the main emphasize was to move away from the Grid approach of handling individual resources, up to a framework, allowing to provide and sell services which represent a combination of different resource types.

2.   Addressing SLAs

Within BREIN, Service Level Agreements are an important piece of the overall BREIN architecture in terms of concepts and component design. SLA Management in this particular case was foreseen to provide the necessary business bits which go beyond the limitations of classical (academic) grid approaches.

Thereby the handling of the SLA lifecycle is addressed by a split in two parts - SLA Management and SLA Representation (cf. Figure 1). Generally speaking, on a conceptual level there should be no dependencies of an SLA Management Framework on a SLA Schema and vice versa. Of course, on the implementation level this statement will become at least partially obsolete.

Figure 2 shows the SLA Lifecycle as addressed by BREIN. For reasons of simplicity, the phase of discovery and negotiation are combined in one phase -

---

[1]BREIN - Business Objective Driven Reliable and Intelligent Grids for Real Business

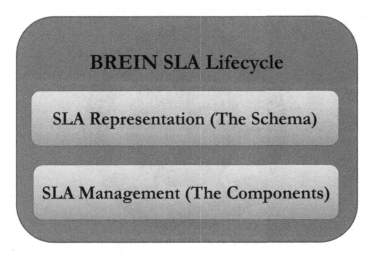

Figure 1. The BREIN SLA concept

creation. The single phases are as follows:

- Development of Service and SLA Templates
- Creation: Discovery and Negotiation of an SLA
- Service Provisioning and deployment
- Execution of the Service
- Assessment and corrective actions during execution (parallel phase to execution of the service)
- Termination and Decommission of the Service

3.   The SLA Schema

3.1   General Issues

In the recent years a set of approaches towards the definition of SLA Schemas have been elaborated, but all of them are still rather in a semi-mature state than product-ready. The two most popular approaches, which also show the highest degree of maturity, are WS-Agreement [2]and WSLA [1]. WSLA, published by IBM, aimed to provide a specification for the definition and monitoring of Service Level Agreements within a Web Service environment. It was published in 2003 but there were no more updates following.

WS-Agreement, which is a specification developed within the Grid Resource

Figure 2.   The different phases of the SLA lifecycle

Allocation Agreement Protocol Working Group of OGF[2] (GRAAP-WG), provides a protocol for establishing agreement on the usage of services between a service provider and a consumer. Version 1.0 of this specification was published in 2007. It defines a language and protocol to represent: the services of providers, create agreements based on offers and aims for monitoring the agreement compliance at runtime.

BREIN follows the approach of merging WS-Agreement and WSLA (cf. Figure 3 which was already investigated in the TrustCoM [3]project. WS-Agreement is taken to set the frame and basic structure of the SLA, whilst WSLA is taken to describe the respective SLA parameters, metrics and how they are measured.

3.2   Semantic Annotations

As mentioned in the introduction, BREIN decided to integrate Multiagent and Semantic Web concepts where applicable to enhance the support of eBusiness end users in setting up and maintaining their business relationships. In previous activities with regard to SLA and their management, it became obvious, that existing solutions work fine, once the involved entities base their messages on a common language with common terminology.

However, if they use different terminologies, especially the discovery of services and the negotiation of an agreement will become nearly impossible. Also different Service Providers offering the same kind of service could loose competitiveness due to use of different terms, describing the same service capabilities.

---

[2]The Open Grid Forum, Website: http://www.ogf.org

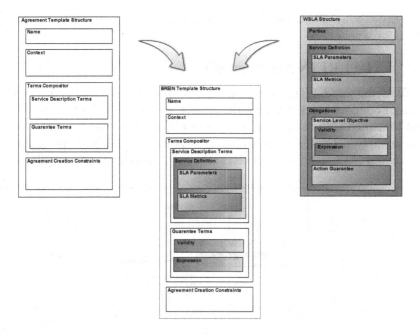

Figure 3. The BREIN SLA Template integrating parts of WS-Agreement and WSLA

Therefore it becomes obvious, that a grid for business such as BREIN needed to enhance the interpretation capabilities of SLA Management components to allow for automated processing of service requests, service offers and service (level) agreements.

Intentionally, BREIN has chosen to build its respective developments on top of an existing specification, namely WS-Agreement as the definition of a completely new specification or an adaptation of an existing would have increased the danger of getting more interoperability problems. With this, backward compatibility is ensured which is an important indicator for future uptake. If an annotation is found, additional reasoning is feasible, if not the SLA document is proceeded as planned.

The whole specification is called 'Semantic Annotated Service Level Agreements' - SA-SLA [4], [5]. An example is given in the listing below. The annotation hereby carries a reference to a concept in a semantic model (in this case the BREIN Business Ontology) that provides a high level description of a Quality of Service metric which can be interpreted by the Negotiation Broker in a meaningful way.

```
<SLAParameter name="Total Cost" type="double" unit="Euro"
  satsla:modelReference="http://eu-brein.com/ontology/Upper/
  QoS#Cost">
```

```
<Metric>Total Cost Metric</Metric>
</SLAParameter>
```

4.   The BREIN Architecture

To set the scene, Figure 4 presents an overview of the overall BREIN architectural building blocks. Within the project, each of this blocks was refined and contained at the end a set of components, enabling the respective block functionalities. Looking at this Figure, it is obvious, that SLA Management is a central block, with connection to all other components. The BREIN SLA

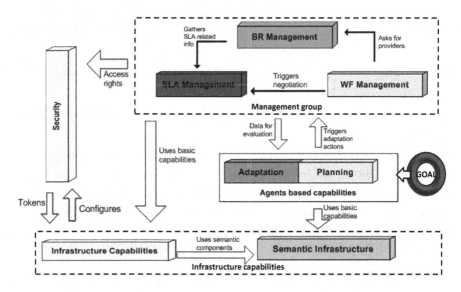

Figure 4.   The overall BREIN Architecture

Architecture, as detailed presented in the official public BREIN architecture deliverable [6]covers all different phases of the SLA Lifecycle. As a detailed description of the design and the functionalities of the SLA Framework would exceed the limit of this paper, this section will only present as example the architectural set up as needed for discovery and negotiation, respectively the creation phase. Thereby the main focus will lie on the enhancements of functionalities by integrating Multiagent and Semantic concepts.

4.1   Creation

Creation of Service Level Agreements in BREIN targets to allow for enhanced discovery of services (and their provider) on basis of SLA capabilities. To allow simple access, the goal was to enable Customers to define their requirements in 'their preferred' language whilst the system is able to understand these terms and to perform discovery accordingly. This shall prevent to put the burden of learning the used SLA language on the end users of the system.

Furthermore, BREIN provides the capability of dynamic negotiation of QoS terms on architectural level. This allows for applying different types of negotiation protocols - from discrete offer negotiation (single phase) to multi-round (multiphase) negotiation. In the respective domains of Service Consumer and Service Provider, the decision is taken (or at least supported, depending on the preference of the user) if a service may be offered and under which circumstances (parameters, payment, etc). This allows for optimized negotiation, taking into account business goals and business policies and also enabling actions like intentional violation of Service Level Agreements in case of overlapping priorities.

The respective architecture is shown in Figure 5. I Without integration of se-

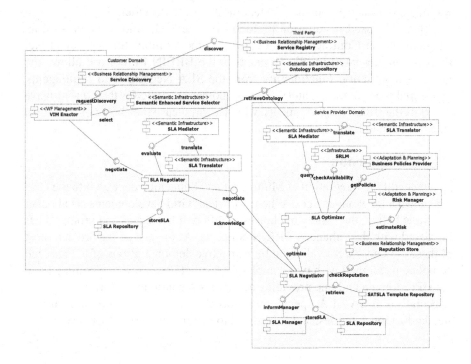

Figure 5. The Creation Architecture

mantic aware components, these enhancement would not be possible. They are the key enabler for a 'common basis' of term exchanges. Namely they are, as seen in Figure 5: hancements are:

- SLA Translator - a semantic component which is an ontology repository for local domain ontologies. Every domain has an own SLA Translator instance.

- SLA Mediator - a semantic component which is able to match SA-SLA requests and offers by converting SLA documents to the local model. It either gets the needed ontology from the SLA Translator or, in case the ontology is not available, it queries a third party ontology repository. Every domain has an own SLA Mediator instance.

- Ontology Repository - a semantic component, which is similar to the SLA Translator an ontology repository. Here Customer and Service Provider can register/store their ontologies to allow retrieval for others, in case they want to interact with them.

In terms of flexibility in negotiation, BREIN provides the optional usage of Multiagents to act on behalf of Customer/Service Provider. By this, the list of potentially used negotiation protocols is extended, amongst others, to an adaption of the Contract Net Protocol [7]- the Combinatorial Contact Net Protocol as presented in [8]. In practice, the BREIN framework allows the move of negotiation functionality from the SLA Negotiator to Multiagents, whilst making it not mandatory. This is another example for the non-intrusive nature of the BREIN developments, which always leave the choice of additional enhanced capabilities up to its end users.

5.   Conclusion

In general the integration of Multiagent and Semantic concepts into the Grid has shown a lot of advantages. Where 'classical' Grid developments acted rather inflexible before, the variety of choices of different languages and protocols has increased with the enhanced BREIN concepts. At the end of the project, most of these concepts were validated by respective demonstrations of the realized components aligned with two completely distinct use cases, one coming from the HPC domain and one providing a logistics scenario at an Airport.
Especially the SA-SLA specification has the potential to influence current standardization activities, and is intended to be brought in the respective bodies.

References

[1] A. Keller and H. Ludwig. The WSLA framework: Specifying and monitoring service level agreements for web services. Journal of Network and Systems Management, Vol. 11, pages 57–81,March 2003.

[2] A. Andrieux, H. Ludwig, et al., Web Services Agreement Specification (WS-Agreement), Technical Report, Open Grid Forum - Grid Resource Allocation and Agreement Protocol Working Group, 2007.

[3] M. Wilson, A. Arenas, and L. Schubert, D63 - Trustcom Framework V4, Technical Report, The TrustCoM Project, 2007

[4] I. Kotsiopoulos, I. Soler Jubert, A. Tenschert, J. Benedicto Cirujeda, and B. Koller. Using Semantic Technologies to Improve Negotiation of Service Level Agreements. In Exploiting the Knowledge Economy - Issues, Applications, Case Studies, Vol. 5 (eChallenges 2008, Stockholm, Sweden, October 2008), IIMC International Information Management Corporation, pages 1045–1052, 2008.

[5] I. Kotsiopoulos, H. Munoz Frutos, B. Koller, S. Wesner, and J. Brooke. A lightweight semantic bridge between Clouds and Grids. In Proceedings of the eChallenges 2009 Conference (eChallenges 2009, Istanbul, Turkey, October 2009), IIMC International Information Management Corporation, 2009. ISBN: 978-1-905824-13-7.

[6] G. Laria and other members of the BREIN consortium, Final Brein Architecture - D4.1.3 V2.Website: http: www.gridsforbusiness.eu, July 2009.

[7] FIPA Contract Net Interaction Protocol Specification, http://www.fipa.org/specs/fipa00029

[8] P. Karaenke and S. Kirn. A Multi-tier Negotiation Protocol for Logistics Supply Chains, Proceedings of the 18th European Conference on Information Systems (ECIS 2010), Pretoria, South Africa, June 7-9, 2010.

NEGOTIATION AND MONITORING OF SERVICE LEVEL AGREEMENTS*

Thomas B. Quillinan
D-CIS Lab
Thales Research and Technology
Delft, The Netherlands
thomas.quillinan@d-cis.nl

Kassidy P. Clark, Martijn Warnier, Frances M.T. Brazier
Systems Engineering
Faculty of Technology, Policy and Management
Delft University of Technology
The Netherlands
[k.p.clark, m.e.warnier, f.m.brazier] @tudelft.nl

Omer Rana
School of Computer Science/Welsh eScience Centre
Cardiff University, UK
o.f.rana@cs.cardiff.ac.uk

Abstract   Service level agreements (SLAs) provide a means to define specific Quality of Service (QoS) guarantees between providers and consumers of services. Negotiation and definition of these QoS characteristics is an area of significant research. However, defining the actions that take place when an agreement is violated is a topic of more recent focus. This paper discusses recent advances in this field and propose some additional features that can help both consumers and producers during the enactment of services. These features include the ability to (re)negotiate penalties in an agreement, and specifically focuses on the renegotiation of penalties during enactment to reflect ongoing violations.

Keywords: monitoring, penalties, negotiation, automation, ws-agreement

---

*This paper extends preliminary work reported at the 5TH INTERNATIONAL WORKSHOP ON GRID ECONOMICS AND BUSINESS MODELS [12]

P. Wieder et al. (eds.), *Grids and Service-Oriented Architectures for Service Level Agreements,*
DOI 10.1007/978-1-4419-7320-7_15, © Springer Science+Business Media, LLC 2010

1.   Introduction

A Service Level Agreement (SLA) is an agreement between clients and providers in the context of a particular service provision. SLAs may be between two parties, for instance, a single client and a single provider, or between multiple parties, for example, a single client and multiple providers. SLAs specify Quality of Service (QoS) properties that must be maintained by a provider during service provision – generally defined as a set of Service Level Objectives (SLOs). Often an SLA is only relevant when a client *directly* invokes a service (rather than through an intermediary – such as a broker). Such direct interaction also implies that the SLOs need to be measurable, and must be monitored during the provision of the service.

Significant work exists on how SLOs may be specified and monitored, such as [7]. Furthermore, some work has focused on actually identifying how SLOs may be impacted by the choice of specific penalty clauses [3, 12, 13]. A trusted mediator may be necessary to resolve conflicts between involved parties. The outcome of conflict resolution depends on the situation: penalties, impact on potential future agreements between the parties and the mandatory re-running of the agreed service, are examples. While it may seem reasonable to penalize SLA non-compliance, there are a number of concerns when issuing such penalties. For example, determining whether the service provider is the only party that should be penalized, or determining the type of penalty that is applied to each party.

Automating conflict resolution processes can provide substantial benefits. In general, there are two main approaches for contractual penalties in SLAs: reputation based mechanisms [1, 5] and monetary fines. It is useful to note that often obligations within an SLA are primarily centered on the provider towards the client. An SLA is therefore an agreement between the provider to offer particular QoS to a client for some monetary return. This paper does not consider scenarios where there is also an obligation on the client towards the provider. An example of such a scenario could be where a provider requires the client to make input data available by a certain time frame to ensure that a particular execution time target is met. If the client is unable to meet the deadline for making such data available, the penalty incurred by the provider would no longer apply. However, similar techniques to those outlined in this paper will apply. Moreover, this paper assumes the Grid's client/provider division of tasks, but could also be extended to apply to agreements between two independent entities.

An aspect of penalizing violations of existing agreements that has not received much attention is how agreements could, or should, be renegotiated during the enactment of the service. A graduated response to violations, as proposed by [12], functions as a post facto reaction to the violation that allows some level of violations with a lesser penalty. Alternatively, providing a renegotiation mechanism has specific advantages: for example, graduated responses can lead to implicit incentives for bad behavior, up to the threshold. For example, if the provider had the option to provision a second consumer knowing that the graduated penalty would be less that the reward for a second service provisioning. In contrast, a renegotiation mechanism allows a more reactive system, where if conditions have altered, producers and consumers can alter the agreement to match those conditions.

In this paper, a number of recent proposals (from [3, 8, 12, 13]) in the area of service violations and penalties negotiation, as well as suggesting approaches that could be used to support renegotiation of SLAs during enactment. The remainder of this paper is organized as follows: Section 2 discusses WS-Agreement and how it can be used to formulate agreements between clients and providers. Monitoring these agreements is discussed in Section 3, where different methodologies are examined. Violations of SLAs is examined in Section 4 and a number of proposals for the future of SLA negotiation and penalties are offered. Finally, Section 5 concludes the paper.

2.   Background

WS-Agreement [2] provides a specification for defining SLAs, and is undergoing standardization by the Open Grid Forum (OGF). WS-Agreement is an XML document standard, that is, interactions between clients and providers are performed using an XML standardized format. There are two types of XML documents in WS-Agreement: *templates* and *agreements*. One basic element is that agreements need to be confirmed by both parties. Including penalties in a WS-Agreement, for example, cannot be one-sided. The WS-Agreements needs to be confirmed by the client. The existing WS-agreement specification, however, will need to be extended to include this step. Mobach *et. al.* [9] proposed such an extension in the context of the WS-Agreement specification.

Figure 1 shows the extended interactions between a service provider (SP) and a consumer (C) described by [9]. The advertisement phase uses WS-Agreement template documents; the request and offer phases also use WS-Agreement agreement documents. Templates describe the different services that the provider supports. When a negotiation takes place, the service provider sends these templates to the consumer. The consumer then makes an offer to the provider and, if acceptable, the agreement is created by the provider based on the offer. In Figure 1, the initial template is generate by the provider, in accordance with the WS-Agreement specification.

Templates and agreements both use the concept of negotiation *terms*. Terms define the service description and guarantees about the service. Guarantees are

1. SP → C   : Advertisement
2. C   → SP : Request
3. SP → C   : Offer
4. C   → SP : Acceptance/Rejection

Figure 1.   Negotiation using WS-Agreement

made relating to the service, such as the quality of service and/or the resource availability during service provision.

Agreements have a name defined by the provider and a context that contains meta-information about the agreement. This meta-information can include identifiers for the service provider and the agreement initiator; the name of the template that the agreement is based on; references to other agreements, and the duration of the agreement [9], as agreements have a fixed period when they are valid. Functional and non-functional requirements are specified in the *Terms* section. This is divided into the *Service Description Terms* (SDT) and *Guarantee Terms* (GT). A SDT holds the functional requirements for the delivery of services, and may refer to one or more components of functionality within one or more services. There may be any number of SDTs in a single agreement. GTs hold a list of services that the guarantee applies to, with the conditions that this guarantee applies, and any potential pre-conditions that must exist.

3.   Monitoring Violations in SLAs

Monitoring plays an important role in determining whether an SLA has been violated, and thereby determine the penalty clause that should be invoked as a consequence. From a legal point of view, monitoring appears as a pre-requisite for contract enforcement. The basic requirement is a set of 'consequences' for breaching the agreed SLOs. Service clients base their trust in service providers largely on the provided monitoring infrastructure.

Monitoring facilitates a direct and automated SLA enforcement mechanism at run-time and without undue delay (that is, once a SLA violation is recorded, the agreed sanction can be automatically triggered). Monitoring also facilitates a more traditional enforcement. In either case, if the provider or the client contests the automatic sanction imposed, it can use monitoring data to argue its case. It is therefore vital to monitor all those metrics that have legal relevance and to give the parties the possibility to retrieve such data in a format that is admissible as evidence.

Identification of violations is either discovered through online monitoring or post facto auditing of the service enactment. However, while auditing allows definitive decisions to be made, it is necessary that accurate logs are maintained by the parties.

3.1   Online Monitoring

Monitoring an agreement requires periodically testing whether the agreement terms have been met by all relevant parties. Depending on the agreement terms, this either entails testing a specific variable, such as network latency, or logging communication between consumer and provider. Monitoring intervals are specified appropriately, such as daily or hourly, depending on the duration of the agreement and the nature of the agreement terms. Monitoring must also support both simple and complex evaluation formulae. For instance, some requirements can be verified by measuring a single variable, such as '*Host is reachable*'. However, other requirements can only be verified once a set of measurements have been performed and their results stored, such as '*Host uptime is greater than 99%*'.

A monitoring mechanism must take accurate measurements and be secure against malicious parties, including the parties with whom agreements have been reached. For instance, a log of communication should not be write accessible to the parties involved: a secure logging mechanism [4] is required. Non-repudiation is also of importance to prove that certain messages were sent by a certain party, and a mechanism to prevent forged messages containing false timestamps or false measurements from being inserted into the message log is also required.

Furthermore, where a monitoring module is placed has to do with trust and objectivity. [12] distinguishes three possible locations for monitoring:

- **Trusted Third Party (TTP)**: an independent module that can monitor (and log) all communication between consumers and service providers. Once the SLA is successfully completed, both parties receive a signed ticket from the TTP that can be used for non-repudiation and/or reputation building of the service provider. However, a TTP cannot measure the internal state of either the consumer or provider.

- **Trusted Module at service provider**: functionally equivalent to a TTP but with access to the internal state of the service provider. However, the provider may not reveal all of the internal state or may report incorrect information to the monitor. A module at this location can show that the provider attempted to avoid violations and dealt with them responsibly when they occurred.

- **Trusted Module on the consumer site**: functionally equivalent to a TTP but it can be difficult to distinguish between provider delay and network delay. A module at this location is not particularly useful for measurements, but only for establishing the trust level for certain providers.

An alternative to this online monitoring approach is to reactively monitor agreements [8]. Reactive monitoring takes place when one of the parties involved in the enactment 'complains' to the monitor that violations are taking place. Such a scheme has the advantage of allowing an immediate response to violations, without the overhead of monitoring every active service provisioning. In the worst case using the approach of [8] entails the same overhead as an online monitoring mechanism.

Passive monitoring is an offline monitoring scheme that uses cryptographic primitives to prove that specified checkpoints in the enactment have been reached correctly. Reactive monitoring extends such a passive monitor, in that, should a checkpoint not be reached, the monitor reacts and starts actively monitoring the enactment from that point forward.

3.2   Violations and Penalties

When a violation occurs, typically a penalty is incurred as a consequence. Penalties can be as simple as terminating the current agreement and finding a different provider, or more complex reputation or monetary based penalties [11]. These penalties are commonly used for service provisioning [6]. In these systems, reputation is a community-wide metric of an entity's trustworthiness. This metric increases if the entity completes transactions without violating the agreement. Conversely, the metric decreases if a term is violated. Reputation based penalties utilize the notion that consumers prefer providers with a higher reputation and try to avoid providers with a lower reputation. In contrast, monetary based penalties operate on the assumption that consumers pay less for poor service and more for better service.

Both of these mechanisms require additional infrastructure and security measures [6]. A reputation based system requires a persistent record of all transactions, both successful and violated. A monetary based system requires a secure means of payment, whether in currency or credit, that has actual value to the users of the system. Both of these approaches require a means of guaranteeing that identities are unique, persistent and legitimate, as well as a conflict resolution process. For instance, underlying authentication mechanisms using a PKI can verify that users are indeed whom they claim to be.

Deposits with a jointly agreed TTP can be used in a monetary based system to implement penalties if needed. In the event of violation, the deposit can be used to effectuate penalty payment. The exact penalty terms can be separately negotiated during SLA negotiation or according to known policies, such as the following [12]:

- **All-or-nothing provisioning**: provisioning of a service must meet all SLOs. ALL of the SLO constraints MUST be met to satisfy the SLA;

- **Partial provisioning**: provisioning of a service must meet some SLOs. SOME of the SLO constraints MUST be met to satisfy the SLA;

- **Weighted Partial provisioning**: provision of a service meets SLOs that have a weighting GREATER THAN a [user specified] threshold.

For example, the SLA framework in AgentScape [10] has been extended to support monitoring and penalty enforcement [3]. A trusted monitoring module is required to measure the provided services and ensure that the GTs in the SLA are being fulfilled by both parties. In addition to this trusted monitoring module, the SLA document must be extended to include monitoring and penalty clauses, similar to those described in [14]. This includes specifying the item to be measured, time constraints, and the method to be used for measurement as described the following example.

Negotiation of the violation policy is also required to determine, for example, the severity of a violation and appropriate action using the policies introduced above. [12] proposes negotiating this violation policy as a separate SDT during the negotiation phase.

4.   Negotiation of Penalties

While negotiations can be managed in the existing WS-Agreement framework, this does not adequately reflect the complexity of penalty negotiation. For example, if a mutually trusted third party cannot be agreed upon by both consumer and provider, there is little point in proceeding with the SLA negotiation. Similarly, if an SLA cannot be agreed upon, there is no need to negotiate the penalty clause. Therefore it is instead proposed to separate these three stages into distinct negotiation steps. Each of these steps follows the same steps as shown in Figure 1: Advertisement; Request; Offer, and Acceptance/Rejection. These steps can be considered negotiations for three separate services.

For example, negotiations to select a TTP proceeds as follows: In the *Creation Constraint* section of the WS-Agreement template, the TTPs trusted by the service provider are listed. When the consumer receives this template, it creates an agreement offer specifying the TTP that they have selected. The offer is then processed by the provider. If it is acceptable, the provider produces the agreement document. This is passed to the consumer for acceptance/rejection. Negotiations for the SLAs and penalties are handled using the same process.

One concern with this approach is the verification that a SLA template refers to the TTP agreement previously negotiated and, similarly, the penalty template to the SLA and TTP agreements. This is achieved by the use of the references to the prior agreements within the *context* section of proceeding templates and agreements. Each penalty agreement then contains references to the TTP and SLA agreements. This ensures that a verifiable link is maintained throughout the service negotiation and provision.

Another approach to the multi-step process could be to specify the template and agreement documents as a single document, with separate services for each of the three stages. This would eliminate the need for three separate negotiations. However, this approach would make the templates more complicated.

4.1   Multiround Negotiation

While negotiation of penalties may become a standard part of SLA negotiations, it is an area where multiple rounds of negotiation has potential to be particularly useful. Several proposals are under consideration by the GRAAP working group of the Open Grid Forum (OGF) towards supporting multiround negotiation. One possible approach is to allow 'negotiation offers'. Such offers would form a non-binding template offering suggestions what *might* be acceptable to the offering party. Such offers would form part of a session where multiple rounds of offers could be provided by one or both parties without altering the fundamental principles of WS-Agreement. Such an approach has the advantage of allowing a rollback mechanism. As each offer forms part of a session and each session has a unique identifier within the negotiation, if negotiations are diverging, the parties would have the option to revert to a previous session.

Multiround negotiations have the potential to allow agreement to be reached on both the service QoS details as well as any penalty clauses. Session based negotiation also has the advantage of allowing both the functional and non-functional aspects to be negotiated seperately, where options could be negotiated, such as, "service *x* with deadline *200*, penalty *$50*, price *$200*" or "service *x* with deadline *500*, penalty *$10*, price *$100*". This would allow much more flexibility to both the provider and consumer. However, no such multiround negotiation mechanism exists within the current WS-Agreement specification.

4.2   Renegotiation

While current work focuses on penalizing violations of SLAs, one alternative approach is to *renegotiate* the SLA during enactment. For example, such an approach would allow the producer and consumer to alter the SLA towards providing a more realistic deadline for the consumer and potentially reducing any penalties that the producer would otherwise be subject. Such a mechanism could take advantage of multiround sessions that formed part of the original negotiation. For example, if a previous round had a longer deadline, at a lower price, the renegotiation might take the form of both parties agreeing to select this SLA session as a replacement. However, this would entail both parties storing the entire set of negotiation sessions until after provisioning has been completed.

Another approach to renegotiation would be for a new round of negotiations to take place during the enactment of the service. An example of this approach would use a version of the existing WS-Agreement negotiation framework, with the initial positions reflecting the current state of the enactment. This renegotiation process could form the penalty associated with an existing SLA. This would allow the enactment to proceed without explicit penalties. Such an approach has the advantage of allowing implicit *penalties* to be negotiated only when required and making these penalties reflect the exact situation rather than the more abstract penalties that would be determined beforehand.

5.   Discussion and Conclusion

The use of penalties in SLAs has obvious benefits for both clients and service providers. Monetary sanctions (and optionally reputation based mechanisms) can be used as, pre-agreed, penalties. Both of these approaches require the participation of a Trusted Third Party. The types of monitoring infrastructure that can be used to validate SLOs during service provisioning are identified. As monetary sanctions are the *de facto* standard in industry for penalty clauses, these are preferred over reputation based solutions, though the latter can be used if so required.

While explicit penalties can be specified within the WS-Agreement framework, they lack flexibility when unexpected events interrupt enactment. This paper discusses the use of both multiround negotiation and runtime renegotiation of SLAs towards improving the experience for both service providers and consumers. While such mechanisms are, as yet, undefined, they indicate an interesting area of future research and usability of service level agreements.

Acknowledgments

This work supported by the NLnet Foundation (www.nlnet.nl) and the EU FP7-IST-215890 "ALIVE" project. We are grateful to Dana Cojocarasu (Research Center for Computers and Law, University of Oslo, Norway) for contribution and discussion regarding European law for electronic contracts.

References

[1] The EigenTrust Algorithm for Reputation Management in P2P Networks., Budapest, Hungary, 2003. ACM Press.

[2] A. Andrieux, K. Czajkowski, A. Dan, K. Keahey, H. Ludwig, T. Nakata, J. Pruyne, J. Rofrano, S. Tuecke, and M. Xu, Web Services Agreement Specification (WS-Agreement), Grid Forum Document, GFD.107, The Open Grid Forum, Joliet, Illinois, United States, 2007.

[3] K.P. Clark, M. Warnier, T.B. Quillinan, and F.M.T. Brazier. Secure monitoring of service level agreements. In Proceedings of the Second International Workshop on Organizational Security Aspects (OSA 2010), IEEE, March 2010.

[4] L. Gymnopoulos, S. Dritsas, S. Gritzalis, and C. Lambrinoudakis. GRID security review. Lecture Notes in Computer Science, pages 100–111, 2003.

[5] J. Sabater and C. Sierra Social regret, a reputation model based on social relations. SIGecom Exch., 3(1):44-56, 2002.

[6] A. Jøsang, R. Ismail, and C. Boyd. A survey of trust and reputation systems for online service provision. Decision Support Systems, 43(2):618–644, 2007.

[7] A. Keller and H. Ludwig. The WSLA framework: Specifying and monitoring service level agreements for web services. Journal of Network and Systems Management, 11(1):57–81, March 2003.

[8] D. Khader, J. Padget, and M. Warnier. Reactive monitoring of service level agreements. In In the Service Level Agreements in Grids Workshop proceedings, 2009.

[9] D.G.A. Mobach, B.J. Overeinder, and F.M.T. Brazier. A WS-Agreement based resource negotiation framework for mobile agents. Scalable Computing: Practice and Experience, 7(1):23–36, 2006.

[10] B.J. Overeinder and F.M.T. Brazier. Scalable middleware environment for agent-based Internet applications. In Applied Parallel Computing, LNCS, Vol. 3732, pages 675–679. Springer, Berlin, 2006.

[11] T.B. Quillinan, B.C. Clayton, and S.N. Foley. GridAdmin: Decentralising grid administration using trust management. In Proceedings of the Third International Symposium on Parallel and Distributed Computing (ISPDC04), Cork, Ireland, July 2004.

[12] O. Rana, M. Warnier, T. B. Quillinan, and F. M. T. Brazier. Monitoring and reputation mechanisms for service level agreements. In Proceedings of the 5th International Workshop on Grid Economics and Business Models (GenCon), Las Palmas, Gran Canaria, Spain, Springer Verlag, August 2008.

[13] O. Rana, M. Warnier, T.B. Quillinan, F.M.T. Brazier, and D. Cojocarasu. Managing violations in service level agreements. In the Proceedings of the Usage of Service Level Agreements in Grids Workshop, September 2007.

[14] A. Sahai, V. Machiraju, M. Sayal, L. J. Jin, and F. Casati. Automated sla monitoring for web services. In EEE/IFIP DSOM, pages 28–41. Springer-Verlag, 2002.

Author Index

P. Wieder et al. (eds.), *Grids and Service-Oriented Architectures for Service Level Agreements,*
DOI 10.1007/978-1-4419-7320-7, © Springer Science+Business Media, LLC 2010